THE WRIGHT BROTHERS

THE WRIGHT BROTHERS

INVENTORS OF THE AIRPLANE

BERNARD RYAN, JR.

FRANKLIN WATTS
A Division of Scholastic Inc.
New York Toronto London Auckland Sydney
Mexico City New Delhi Hong Kong
Danbury, Connecticut

For my wife and most beloved friend, Jean Bramwell Ryan

Photographs © 2003: Brown Brothers: 47, 52, 53; Corbis Images: 64, 78, 111 (Bettmann), 113 (Raymond Gehman), 61, 108; From the Collections of The Henry Ford Museum & Greenfield Village: 21 (D12226), 98 (D31905); Holiday Film Corp: back cover, 57; Hulton | Archive/Getty Images: 26, 27, 74, 101; Library of Congress: 6 right, 15, 37, 43, 96; National Park Service: 63; North Wind Picture Archives: 9; Photo Researchers, NY/US Library of Congress: cover background; Smithsonian Institution, Washington, DC: cover foreground, 2; Wright State University, Special Collections and Archives: 6 left, 10, 13, 17, 23, 28, 46, 62, 69, 72, 76, 77, 79, 82, 85, 89, 94, 103.

Library of Congress Cataloging-in-Publication Data

Ryan, Bernard, 1923

The Wright brothers: inventors of the airplane / by Bernard Ryan, Jr.
    p. cm. — (Great life stories)
Includes bibliographical references and index.
Contents: Living, playing, thinking together—Brothers become a team—Thoughts about flying—Roll, pitch, and yaw—Why Kitty Hawk—December 17, 1903—Above the cow pasture—As thick as thieves—Charming all Europe and New York—Pilots, crowds, and profits—Protected by law and mud—Inventing autopilot and popular toy.

ISBN 0-531-12254-9

1. Wright, Orville, 1871–1948—Juvenile literature. 2. Wright, Wilbur, 1867–1912—Juvenile literature. 3. Aeronautics—United States—Biography—Juvenile literature. 4. Inventors—United States—biography—Juvenile literature. 5. Aeronautics—United States—History—Juvenile literature. [1. Wright, Orville, 1871–1948. 2. Wright, Wilbur, 1867–1912. 3. Aeronautics—Biography.] I. Title. II. Series.

TL540.W7R93 2003
629.13'0092'273—dc21

                                                                    2003000954

CONTENTS

ABOVE: Baby Katharine Wright, youngest and only girl among the five Wright children. Before she was school age, her brother Lorin taught her to read.

RIGHT: Wilbur Wright around the time when Orville was born in 1871.

LIVING, PLAYING, AND THINKING TOGETHER

The brothers who invented the airplane were unusual. What made them different from other people was described by Wilbur Wright himself. He once said, "From the time we were little children, my brother Orville and myself lived together, played together, worked together, and, in fact, thought together. We usually owned all of our toys in common, talked over our thoughts and aspirations so that nearly everything that was done in our lives has been the result of conversations, suggestions, and discussions between us."

The boys had older brothers. Reuchlin was ten and Lorin was eight years old when Wilbur was born on April 16, 1867. Wilbur was four and a half years old when Orville was born on August 19, 1871. Their sister, Katharine, was born on Orville's third birthday. The family often called her *Sterchens*, which is German for "little sister."

Home was at 7 Hawthorn Street in Dayton, Ohio, where the children's father, Milton Wright, was a minister of the Church of the United Brethren in Christ and edited the church newspaper. Their great-grandfather had been a pioneer farmer near Dayton, and their mother, Susan, had spent her childhood living on a farm in Indiana.

Orville Wright always remembered visiting his grandfather's farm and seeing, in its carriage shop, a lathe (a woodworking tool) driven by a foot treadle (pedal). He and Wilbur knew their mother had spent hours in that shop. She had an uncommon ability with mechanical things and made many toys for her boys—even a sled they rode down snow-covered hills.

Susan Wright taught her boys to read before they attended school, and it seems likely that they got from her their special skills of picturing their inventions in their mind's eye before actually building them.

The family moved to Cedar Rapids, Iowa, when Milton Wright was appointed to be the bishop of his church. His work took him for long trips westward visiting church members, and the young brothers knew he was always sure to bring home exciting gifts. One they never forgot came in the fall of 1878.

"Father brought home," said Orville many years later, "a small toy which would lift itself into the air." It was similar to a toy made in China and in Europe centuries earlier. In the original toy, you held a hollow tube or spindle. In it you placed a stick with a four-bladed propeller at the top. You wound a string around the end of the stick, yanked the string, and up flew the spinning propeller.

The toy the bishop brought home was even better. Designed by French inventor Alphonse Pénaud, it was made of paper, bamboo, and cork and was powered by a rubber band. In effect, it was a helicopter. Twin propellers shot it up as high as 50 feet (15.2 meters) in the air, or made it fly in circles or float overhead as long as twenty-five seconds. Wilbur and Orville made copies of the Pénaud toy. They flew successfully, but as Orville said later, "When we undertook to build the toy on a much larger scale it failed to work so well."

SCHOOL DAYS BUT NOT IN SCHOOL

When Orville was five years old, his mother walked him to his first day at school. Each morning after that, she sent him off, dressed for school. She welcomed him home on time each afternoon. After several weeks, she learned that her five-year-old son had been walking to his friend Ed Sines's house, spending the day, and coming home at the right time. She then homeschooled him through kindergarten and first grade.

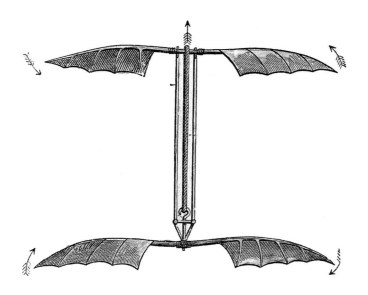

Alphonse Pénaud's toy helicopter, made in 1870. Its propeller blades were gold-plated to increase their efficiency, and small parts were made of aluminum. The next year, Pénaud invented and flew a scale model monoplane (a single-wing airplane) that he called a "Planophore." Its rubber-band motor took it more than 65 yards (60 meters).

This photograph shows Orville at the age of ten in 1881. By this time, he had won first prize in a penmanship class and was handy at building kites to sell to his friends.

In second grade, Orville's teacher noticed him bent over his desk, fooling with pieces of wood. She asked what he was doing. He said he was putting together a flying machine and added that he could fly with his brother if they had a much larger machine.

At the end of second grade, Orville was ready to move to the third-grade reader. But school officials wouldn't promote him without hearing him read aloud from the second-grade reader. He furiously "read" the required text and then let the school officials see he was holding the book upside down. The officials agreed that if he could memorize text that easily, he should be promoted to the next grade.

To earn pocket money, Wilbur worked in his father's newspaper office. When he saw how long it took to fold the papers by hand, he invented and built a folding machine. He and Orville built a 6-foot (1.8 m) wood lathe powered by a treadle (probably like the one they had seen in their grandfather's carriage shop). Orville, only six years old, pulled his wagon door to door to collect bones that he sold to Dayton's fertilizer factory. At ten, when he found that a junkyard would buy pieces of metal and wood, he enlisted his seven-year-old sister to collect scraps in the street. At the same age, a postcard he wrote to his traveling father showed that his mind had plenty of curiosity, although he still had to learn some punctuation. The card said: "The other day I took a machine can and filled it with water then I put it on the stove I waited a little while and the water came squirting out of the top about a foot."

When Orville was in sixth grade, Bishop Wright moved his family to Richmond, Indiana. That spring, in 1883, Orville got into mischief and his teacher suspended him. He didn't tell his parents and he didn't go back to school. At that time, most states did not have laws requiring young people go to school, and there were no truant officers to find Orville and take him back to the classroom.

In June, the family moved back to Dayton. The next fall, Dayton school authorities said Orville would have to repeat sixth grade because the Richmond schools had no record that he had completed it. He was furious,

RULES FOR READING ALOUD

The book Orville held upside down while he "read" was probably *McGuffey's Second Reader*, one of six readers published by the Rev. William Holmes McGuffey between 1841 and 1879. They were introduced in Cincinnati, Ohio, and were soon used in schools across the United States. The third reader, which Orville proved he was ready for, contained rules for reading aloud. Its text is considered suitable for students in today's junior high schools. Many people who now homeschool their children use the *McGuffey Readers*.

saying he would not repeat sixth grade. His mother convinced the school principal he could do the work. The following June, Orville Wright won the prize for being Dayton's best student in mathematics.

Both Wright parents believed strongly in both formal and informal education. Bishop Milton Wright had been a teacher himself before he was married. He knew that learning occurred both in the classroom and out of it. One teacher who had taught several of the Wright children, Esther Wheeler, remembered long afterward that "Bishop Wright did not believe in ten month school, and would tell his boys to take half a day off now and then. He believed that they could keep up with their classes and miss a few days also. His boys were excellent scholars, just as he argued they would be."

Many years after his boyhood, Orville talked about how valuable the atmosphere at 7 Hawthorn Street had been to the growth of his and Wilbur's minds. "We were lucky enough," he recalled, "to grow up in an environment where there was always much encouragement to children to pursue intellectual interests, to investigate whatever aroused curiosity. In a different kind of environment, our curiosity might have been nipped long before it could have borne fruit."

As boys in the 1870s and 1880s, the Wright brothers knew just two kinds of school: elementary and secondary. Elementary school went from first through eighth grade. Its aim was to get students ready to handle the kinds of reading, writing, and arithmetic they would have to cope with in grades nine through twelve of secondary school, better known as "high school." Very little time was spent on subjects that became common in the twentieth century, such as music, art, science, and physical education.

In about 1900, long after the Wrights' schooldays, educators began to understand that eight years of elementary school were too many. They found that six years in elementary, then two or three in junior high, then three or four in high school worked better for students and teachers.

ATHLETE AND PRINTER

In Wilbur's senior year in high school, his average marks for the first three semesters were 94, 96, and 95, and he was not taking easy courses. His schedule included geometry (the mathematics of points, lines, angles, surfaces, and solids), geology (the science of Earth's composition and solid matter, such as rocks), both the Latin and Greek languages, and English composition. These were typical subjects to learn in secondary school, in which the aim was to get students ready for the even harder work of studying in college or in professional schools, such as law or medicine. At that time, however, only about one out of twenty high school students went on to college. The large majority of students left school after tenth or eleventh grade, when they were sixteen or seventeen years old, and went to work. At 7 Hawthorn Street, Wilbur's parents began talking about sending him to Yale University.

Wilbur Wright at seventeen, when he was a high school senior and member of the Class of 1884 in Richmond, Indiana.

Wilbur Wright was not only a fine student, he was also a top-notch athlete who was especially good at gymnastics. He sped around town on a high-wheeled bicycle bought with his own earnings. Playing on his high school football team, he could outrun anybody.

In the winter of 1885, eighteen-year-old Wilbur was in a hockey game when a player's stick caught him in the mouth, knocking him flat on the ice with lips bleeding, teeth broken and knocked out, and gums torn. It took weeks for doctors to fit his damaged gums with false teeth. The accident ended talk of Wilbur's going to Yale or any other college. For three years afterward, he stayed at home, studying ancient and modern history, current events, literature, and science. It is quite likely that Wilbur's regular reading included the magazine *Scientific American*, which has been publishing articles on developments in science and technology since 1845.

At the same time, Wilbur's father was traveling and his mother had become ill with tuberculosis, a disease of the lungs that was common at the time. By 1886, she was an invalid, unable to manage the details of family life.

Wilbur's older brothers had already left home. Reuchlin was married and had a family. Lorin was living in Kansas, making his own life. Orville

AT FIRST, HOCKEY WAS "SHINNY"

First played on the beaches of Galway, Ireland, in the 1400s, hockey became popular in Canada three hundred years later and was played on ice. It developed as a winter sport in the United States after the Amateur Hockey Association of Canada was formed in 1884 (the year before Wilbur's accident) and drew up formal rules. At that time, some players still called the game by its earlier name, "shinny."

and Katharine, who were fifteen and twelve years old, were too young to handle the household. So Wilbur stayed home to care for his mother and provide for his brother and sister. Devoted to his mother, he took full charge of her until she died on July 4, 1889. Then Katharine, who turned sixteen that August, began running the household. As she went on with high school in the fall, she did the shopping and cooking.

Long before that, Orville's mind was stretching beyond the classroom. He was captivated by the line drawings that illustrated magazines. Inspired, he used the spring from a pocket knife to cut printing blocks so deftly that Wilbur bought him woodcutting tools for Christmas.

Orville's longtime pal from kindergarten, Ed Sines, owned a small printing press. They started doing print jobs for eighth-grade classmates, but the press was not good enough to do quality work. Wilbur and Lorin bought them a better machine, and the Sines & Wright print shop's list of customers grew beyond eighth grade. Responding to the boys' boast that they could "do job printing cheaper than any other house in town," Dayton business people ordered business cards, envelopes, letterheads, tickets, advertising circulars, and handbills.

Ed Sines at work in the Wright printing office. Ed was Orville Wright's boyhood pal. Their first newspaper, for eighth-grade classmates, was halted by Orville's father when he saw that one page contained only the name Sines & Wright printed multiple times.

PRINTING AND POPCORN

For two summers, Orville worked in a print shop as an apprentice, becoming a skilled typesetter. Then he and Wilbur rounded up junkyard parts and built a professional press. It could imprint sheets of paper as large as 11 by 16 inches (27.9 by 40.6 centimeters).

Popcorn ended the Sines & Wright partnership. A grocery-store owner owed them two dollars for printing advertising handbills. He paid them with two dollars' worth of popcorn. Ed wanted to eat the popcorn. Orville wanted to resell it to another grocer and use the money to buy extra type, which are tiny metal letters that are set in lines, creating words and sentences. Ed refused. Orville bought Ed's half of the business, becoming sole owner. Ed then worked for the firm for ten years.

Now sixteen years old, Orville built a larger press in 1888, again with junkyard parts. He used an old buggy's folding top to press the type down as each sheet of paper was printed. The press could imprint a newspaper-

DRAWINGS CARVED INTO WOOD

Until the 1890s, illustrations in magazines were made by artists who drew pictures. Photography had not yet come into common use. A favorite medium was wood engraving—the art of carving a picture into a block of very smooth wood by cutting away the area the artist did not want to see printed. The remaining lines were inked in the printing press and reproduced the drawing on paper. Among the popular magazines Orville probably saw regularly at home, and that used woodblock illustrations were *Harper's*, *Scribner's Monthly*, and *The Century*.

sized two-page "spread." Running at full speed, it turned out one thousand pages an hour. Now Orville had a profitable business printing pamphlets, brochures, and annual reports.

CREATING A NEWSPAPER, BUILDING A PORCH

In March of 1889, when he was seventeen years old and a high school junior, Orville started publishing a weekly newspaper, the *West Side News.* He thought people would buy it to keep up with local interests and business. Within two months, it was making a profit. Orville rented business space and moved his operation out of a shed behind the Wright home. He also decided that he would quit school at the end of eleventh grade and not go to college. Wilbur soon became editor of the paper, with Orville as the publisher and printer.

In the spring of 1890, when Orville was eighteen and Wilbur was twenty-three years old, they published a daily, *The Evening Item,* to succeed their weekly paper. The brothers advised advertisers that their daily

The seventeenth issue of the weekly *West Side News.* The price in the upper left corner reads: "Quarter of year, twenty cents; Six weeks, ten cents."

would "boom up business interests and increase the value of West Side property. If there is anyone who does not think it worth a cent a day to have a daily paper here, it must be that he has no property interests in the West Side and does not know how to read."

Dayton already had twelve newspapers. The two best-sellers boasted high-speed presses that churned out advertising inserts and special sections, such as sports for men and household features for women. The Wright brothers could not compete with that. In August of 1890, four months after launching *The Evening Item*, they quit and returned to running their printing plant.

Now the brothers' busy minds decided that 7 Hawthorn Street needed improvements. They bought lumber and went to work building an extensive porch and porch roof across the front of the house and far down one side. With shapely posts and banisters, and just enough gingerbread trim, the porch turned the Wrights' plain, boxlike house into a typical Victorian home. While the brothers had gained much of their mechanical abilities from their mother, it is likely that Orville and Wilbur picked up their home improvement skills from their regular reading. They were probably avid readers of *Manufacturer and Builder*, a popular magazine that described the latest tools, inventions, and techniques. Undoubtedly they also regularly read *Popular Science Monthly*. Since 1872, it had been carrying articles about science and invention by such well-known people as Alexander Graham Bell, Thomas Edison, and Louis Pasteur.

With Ed Sines handling the printing operation, the business was taking care of itself. Orville was beginning to think there might be more to life than printing business cards, letterheads, and handbills. And Wilbur, who had enjoyed being editor of the *West Side News* but was not in love with printing itself, was looking around for something to match his and Orville's skills and talents.

BROTHERS BECOME A TEAM

The brothers did not have to look far for their next endeavor. Wilbur had been riding his high-wheeled bicycle since high school. But high-wheelers, on which the rider sat 4 to 5 feet (1.2 to 1.5 m) above the ground, were dangerous. It took real skill to zoom through crowded streets or along graveled country roads without losing control. They also had solid rubber tires. No wonder high-wheelers were known as "bone-shakers."

In 1892, both Wilbur and Orville bought "safety" bicycles. Invented only five years earlier, they had two wheels of equal size. The rider's feet reached the ground. Instead of pedals attached to the hub of the big wheel, a setup that demanded skillful braking, pedals were attached to a sprocket that turned a chain drive and controlled a "coaster brake."

When Ed Sines organized a cycle club, the brothers competed in races and participated in group rides. Riders soon learned that when anybody's bike needed repair, it was those talented mechanics, the Wright brothers, who could fix it. After all, they were the ones who built printing presses from junkyard parts when they were only schoolboys.

In December of 1892, the brothers opened the Wright Cycle Exchange, repairing bicycles and selling parts, accessories, and new bikes. Bicycles were not cheap. While the typical U.S. worker was earning about $440 a year, a boy's safety bicycle of good quality cost between $40 and $50, and an adult bike cost from $50 to more than $100. The brothers took used bikes as trade-ins, but refused to resell them if their quality was poor.

They had fun. Using two 4-foot (1.2-m) wheels from high-wheelers, they made a giant bicycle built for two. Off they went through Dayton's West Side, leaving spectators doubled over with laughter as the Wright brothers rolled by on their contraption.

THE BICYCLE REVOLUTION OF THE 1890s

The craze for high-wheelers began in 1878 in Hartford, Connecticut. The year 1887 brought the "safety" bike's strong triangular frame, same-size wheels, and inflated tires. By 1890, forty thousand bikes were built annually in the United States, and in 1895, more than three hundred manufacturers produced 1.2 million bicycles. In 1892, the U.S. Patent Office got so busy handling bicycle patents that it created a special department for them. And by 1900, it had issued 7,573 patents for bicycles and their parts.

MONEY, BICYCLES, AND FAMILY

Within a year, Wilbur and Orville had changed the name to the Wright Cycle Company and were making more money selling and repairing bicycles than they made from printing. For eighteen months, they produced a weekly magazine called *Snap-Shots of Current Events* that they loaded with jokes, feature articles, and advertising for Wright Cycle and other stores. When they heard that someone had stolen a forthcoming high school test, they put their prankster sense of humor to work, printing up advertising flyers that looked like test sheets. Each question and answer, however, glorified the merits of Wright Cycle.

After three years, the brothers knew what was good or bad about every bicycle line. They decided that they themselves could manufacture better bikes than most. They built wheels—a customer could order wooden or metal rims—and mechanical

The Wright Cycle Company as it stands today in Greenfield Village, Michigan. Automobile maker Henry Ford moved the building from Dayton in 1937. The 1903 Wright Flyer was built in this bicycle shop.

BIKES VERSUS AUTOMOBILES

While the Wright bicycle business was thriving in 1896, the brothers saw the first "horseless carriage" on Dayton streets. A handmade gasoline-powered buggy was put together by their friend, mechanic "Cordy" Ruse. Wilbur was not impressed. He told Cordy he'd be wise to suspend a bed sheet under the engine to catch the nuts and bolts that kept shaking loose.

parts. They painted every frame with five coats of either red or black baked enamel.

Between 1896 and 1900, customers bought three hundred Wright bicycles. The best-seller, the Wright Special, cost $18—much less than early safety bicycles. The brothers' profit each year was between $2,000 and $3,000, while the print shop's profit was only $218 annually.

Something more important than making money happened to the brothers because of their bicycle business. They became a team. They found they could work, think, and invent together. Their partnership was so close that they kept a joint bank account, where each felt comfortable putting in or taking out money without telling the other.

At home, the brothers, their sister, and their father were a tightly knit family. Bishop Wright believed, however, that a woman had a right to an education and a career. After Katharine graduated from high school in 1892 and spent a year studying at home, he was glad to see her off to Oberlin College.

For four years, with their father traveling and Katharine at college, Wilbur and Orville ran their shop and kept house. They took turns cooking. In a letter to his sister, Wilbur wrote:

Orville's week we have bread and butter and meat and gravy and coffee three times a day. My week I give him more variety. By the end of his week there is a lot of cold meat stored up, so the first half of my week we have bread and butter and "hash" and coffee, and the last half we have bread and butter and eggs and sweet potatoes and coffee.

MOVING MASHED POTATOES

By 1896, Wilbur was twenty-nine, Orville twenty-five, and their sister twenty-two. None of them seemed interested in marriage. They had nieces and nephews living nearby, for their brother Lorin, with his wife and four children, had returned to Dayton from Kansas. They were living only a block away. Years later, Lorin's daughter Leontine recalled that "Grandpa Wright's house was a favorite place. He and my Aunt Katharine and my Uncles Wilbur and Orville spent many days entertaining us there.

This photograph shows a Wright family picnic in about 1915 (clockwise left to right) Orville Wright, Katharine Wright, Milton Wright (son of Lorin), William Jenkins, Jim Jenkins, Horace "Bus" Wright (son of Lorin), Lottia Andrews, Ivonette "Netta" Stokes Wright (wife of Lorin and mother of "Bus" and Milton), and Lorin Wright.

Sometimes there was picture taking, fascinating candy making, good reading sessions, and good games indoors and out."

Another niece, Ivonette, remembered her uncles well. "When my mother had an errand taking her downtown," she said, "we were dropped off at the bicycle shop, and either Orville or Wilbur, or both, baby-sat us. They were never too busy to entertain us."

Orville's candy-making and practical jokes were much loved. "If he ran out of games he would make candy," said Ivonette. "He made fudge with a long thermometer to test how long it should be boiled. It was beaten to the right consistency and it was delicious."

Lorin's youngest child, a son called "Bus," described one of Orville's pranks: "During many of our Sunday dinners they used to tease me as to whether they had enough potatoes, since I always liked mashed potatoes. One Sunday Uncle Orv remarked, 'It seems funny how Bus's plate always makes for the mashed potatoes,' and with that my plate started to move towards the mashed potatoes he was serving. It turned out he had pasted a thread to the bottom of my plate which he pulled toward him."

Best of all, the Wright brothers still liked mechanical toys. "When we were old enough to get toys," said Ivonette, "Uncle Orv and Uncle Will had a habit of playing with them until they were broken, then repairing them so that they were better than when they were bought."

Wilbur and Orville were busy with nieces and nephews and bicycles and printing. But running a couple of small businesses was not enough to keep their inventive minds occupied. More and more, they thought about something they kept reading about in the newspapers.

THREE

THOUGHTS ABOUT FLYING

I n the newspapers, the brothers kept reading about flying. For centuries, humankind had dreamed of taking to the skies. Now more and more people were thinking human flight might be possible.

WOULD-BE FLYERS MAKE NEWS

In September of 1894, Wilbur and Orville read a magazine article about Otto Lilienthal, a German engineer who had made two thousand flights using gliders. Other news reports described experiments that were closer to home. In May of 1896, two scientists were convinced that a successful flying machine could be built. They were Alexander Graham Bell, inventor of the telephone, and Samual Pierpont Langley, secretary (the chief executive) of the Smithsonian Institution. Over ten years, Langley had built one large model flying machine after another that failed to fly. Now he and Bell were topping off that work with a large model whose wings stretched 14 feet (4.3 m) across.

Bell and Langley and their helpers launched the model from atop a houseboat on the Potomac River at Quantico, Virginia. A lightweight steam engine drove twin propellers as the machine skimmed the river's surface. Then, circling twice, it climbed slowly to 100 feet (30.5 m) above the ground in ninety seconds before the steam ran out. Altogether, it flew 3,000 feet (914.4 m) at 20 to 25 miles (32.1 to 40.2 kilometers) per hour.

Bell and Langley were not the only ones in the United States who were determined to fly. Another was Octave Chanute, a talented sixty-four-year-old engineer. He had built the first bridge across the Missouri River. As the United States grew, Chanute had designed railroads, stockyards,

This is the design for a "flying machine" (actually a glider incapable of powered flight) patented in Germany in 1895 by Otto Lilienthal.

and water- and sewage-treatment plants. He had also studied how high winds could destroy suspension bridges and roofs of buildings. Using wind tunnels, he had tested the flow of air along various surfaces.

Chanute thought powered flight could be developed by first experimenting with gliders large enough to carry a man. In June of 1896, he and his assistant, Augustus Herring, and some helpers took their gliders to the wind-swept dunes along the Indiana shore of Lake Michigan. There they could find open areas with strong winds. Shortly afterwards, *The Chicago Tribune* reported Chanute's first successful flight, and Chanute's experiments became front-page news across the United States.

Reports on Lilienthal, Langley, and Chanute stirred the brothers' imaginations. Orville, the artisan who could make or repair anything, was eager for a new challenge. Wilbur, the reader, editor, and quiet student, was always ready to mull over the possibilities promised by new ideas. Knowing he could learn only so much by reading countless news stories about flying

In 1896, Octave Chanute's followers flew five-wing gliders above the dunes on the Lake Michigan shore.

experiments, he began his own studies. He found desolate hills beyond Dayton where powerful updrafts attracted many soaring birds. There he lay on his back studying, through strong binoculars, how they used their wings and tails to control their paths through the air.

ORVILLE NEARLY DIES

In August of 1896, Katharine Wright was about to return to Oberlin College to start her junior year. But Orville was sick. His fever reached 105.5 degrees Fahrenheit (41.2 degrees Celsius), which is an extremely high temperature for a fever. His doctor found he had typhoid fever, and that meant there was little any doctor could do except wait and see if the patient's system could fight off the disease.

Katharine delayed her return to Oberlin. Orville's fever dropped to 103 degrees Fahrenheit (39.8° C) but stayed there. For a month, he suffered from delirium, a condition in which his speech made little sense and he was seeing things that were not there. Day and night, Wilbur and Katharine took

This photograph shows Katharine Wright as an Oberlin student in 1896. After college, she lived at home with her father and brothers Wilbur and Orville while she taught English and Latin at Dayton's Steele High School.

Typhoid Fever

Typhoid fever was common for centuries, but has become rare in places with modern plumbing and sanitation. It is caused by the typhoid bacillus, a tiny organism that cannot be seen without a microscope. The bacillus lives in human waste. Where sanitation is poor, it can pass into well water or into foods and drinks handled by humans. It is easily spread by common flies and by unwashed hands. At the time of Orville's illness, typhoid fever killed about one out of every five people who came down with it.

People who do not themselves have the disease can carry it and pass it on to others. They are called "carriers." In 1900, after major epidemics of typhoid fever in Chicago and Philadelphia and long after Orville's illness, the first vaccination against it was developed.

turns feeding him beef broth and milk, giving him cold sponge baths to reduce his fever, and reading to him.

Late in August, Wilbur read a report that Otto Lilienthal had lost control while flying his glider in Germany. He had hit the ground from an altitude of 50 feet (15.2 m) and died the next day. "The notice of his death," Wilbur said later, "aroused a passive interest which had existed from my childhood, and led me to take down from the shelves of our home library a book on *Animal Mechanism* which I had already read several times."

The book did not give Wilbur much useful information. It contained pictures of birds in flight but did not explain how they did what they did.

When Orville felt better, Wilbur told him about Lilienthal, and they talked about flying. "We could not understand that there was anything about a bird that could not be built on a larger scale and used by man,"

Orville said later. "If the bird's wings would sustain it in the air without any muscular effort, we did not see why man could not be sustained by the same means."

Wilbur later said, "Our own growing belief that man might learn to fly was based on the idea that while thousands of the most dissimilar body structures, such as insects, fish, reptiles, birds and mammals, were flying every day at pleasure, it was reasonable to suppose that man might also fly."

It was time to do something to test this idea.

ROLL, PITCH, AND YAW

On May 30, 1899, Wilbur wrote to the Smithsonian Institution:

My observations have convinced me that human flight is practicable. It is only a question of knowledge and skill. . . . I wish to obtain such papers as the Smithsonian Institution has published on this subject, and if possible a list of other works in print in the English language. I am an enthusiast, but not a crank in the sense that I have some pet theories as to the proper construction of a flying machine.

The Smithsonian Institution sent a list of books on "aerial navigation," including works by Chanute and Langley, and four pamphlets on flying experiments. Studying the material, Orville said later, "We found that

Lilienthal had been killed through his inability to balance his machine in the air. We set to work to devise a more efficient means of maintaining the equilibrium."

NEEDED FOR FLIGHT: THREE BASICS

The more he read and thought, the more Wilbur was convinced that everyone's previous thinking about flying had been guesswork. Nobody had yet come up with a machine that met what he and Orville considered the three basic needs of flight. First, their invention would need a wing that could lift the machine into the air. It would also need an engine with enough power to move the machine fast enough so the rush of air over the wings would create the needed lift. Finally, it would have to have a system that controlled the machine's direction.

The first two were not so difficult. The wings of Lilienthal's and Chanute's gliders, and of Langley's Aerodromes, provided an upward force, or

AN ENGLISHMAN'S GIFT

Englishman James Smithson died in 1829, leaving $550,000 to the United States. His will said he wanted to establish an institution "for the increase and diffusion of knowledge."

By 1896, the Smithsonian Institution was a leader in learning and research, with vast collections of historical objects, technological inventions, and art housed in several museums and galleries, as well as an extensive zoo.

"lift." Langley's light steam engines proved that power could drive wings into the air, and lightweight gasoline engines were being built and improved daily.

The third problem—controlling direction—was tough. No machine that had to be controlled in three directions at once had ever been built. But that was what was needed, and Wilbur's bicycle experience helped his thinking. The three directions, and the terms by which they later became known by airplane pilots, were roll, pitch, and yaw.

Thinking about them, Wilbur imagined riding his bicycle. Roll was the motion to either side as he leaned his bike to make a turn. Pitch was like riding uphill or downhill. The flying machine would pitch upward to rise or downward to descend. Yaw was when the machine flew along a straight line, but its position was skewed to the left or right, like walking along a line while the head and shoulders were turned to look left or right.

Wilbur knew that yaw could be controlled with a vertical rudder, and pitch with a horizontal rudder, or elevator, that pushed the nose or tail of the machine up or down. But controlling roll was much more difficult. He kept thinking about how to control the roll of a flying machine.

A BOX SHOWS THE WAY

At the Wright bicycle shop one evening in the summer of 1899, Wilbur was selling a new inner tube for a bicycle tire. He took the tube from its long cardboard box. Chatting with his customer, he happened to twist the ends of the box in opposite directions. When he twisted the near right corner downward, the near left corner went upward, and vice versa. At once it occurred to him that the wings of a flying machine could be twisted in the same way to control the machine's horizontal level.

Wilbur took the box home and showed Orville and Katharine how the upper and lower wings of a flying machine could be warped so the air flowing over them would force one end up and the other end down.

The brothers began building a glider-shaped kite with upper and lower wings each measuring 5 feet (1.5 m) across. At the front of each end of each wing, they attached cords running to sticks held upright in each hand by the person flying the kite. Wilbur took the glider-kite to a field where Ed Sines and Orville had flown kites as boys. There several school-boys were intrigued by seeing a grown man make a large double-winged kite dive, climb, and roll.

Wilbur flew that kite only once. He and Orville agreed it was time to build a human-carrying glider that used the same wing-warping method. But first they had to figure out how to shape the wings to provide enough lift to carry the weight of the machine with a man aboard it.

THE SECRET OF WING SHAPE

Wilbur found that English engineer John Smeaton had studied how the blades of a windmill work. In 1759, he had written reports on air pressure and blade shapes. Smeaton had also studied the wings of birds. Naturalists knew that any bird's wings were arched from the front, or leading, edge to the back, or trailing, edge. This arch was called "camber," from the French word *cambrer*, meaning "to arch, bend, or curve." Smeaton found that, moving through the air, a cambered surface had more lift than a flat surface. He didn't know *why* it had more lift—nor did anyone else until about twenty-five years after the Wrights first flew—but he knew it did.

THE LIFT THAT MAKES IT FLY

What nobody knew until years later was that any wing's camber makes the air dashing over it move faster and farther than the air passing under it. This creates less air pressure above the wing than beneath it, producing a vacuum above the wing. A vacuum is defined as "an emptiness of space," meaning that there is nothing there—not even air. The wing cannot resist rising into that empty space.

After Smeaton's reports were written, engineers had studied the resistance, or "drag," that various shapes had against the wind. Using wind tunnels, they had developed mathematical formulas to predict how much lift and drag would be produced in various wind speeds by several wing shapes (also called *airfoils*).

The Wright brothers found that, although both Lilienthal and Chanute designed wings that flew, the camber they used was the simple arc of a circle, with its highest point exactly halfway between the wing's leading and trailing edges. The Wrights decided to move the high point of the arc much closer to the leading edge of the wing. This would allow thinner camber—roughly half the thickness of the others' designs—and less drag, or resistance to the air.

One question was how large to make the wing surface. The glider would weigh 50 pounds (22.7 kilograms), and Wilbur weighed 140 pounds (63.5 kg), so the wing had to lift 190 pounds (86.2 kg). Using formulas from Lilienthal and Chanute, he calculated that a wing in a 15-mile (24-km)-per-hour wind could generate enough lift to carry 190 pounds (86.2 kg) aloft if its surface area totaled 204.75 square feet (19.04 square meters). To make it easier to build, the brothers divided the area into upper and lower wings.

WANTED: WIND, NOT WATCHERS

Now the brothers wondered where they could find winds that blew steadily at 15 or 16 miles (25.7 km) per hour. No field around Dayton had winds like that all day and every day. Remembering that Chanute had flown in steady winds on the Indiana Dunes, Wilbur wrote to the U.S. Weather Bureau. It sent him a report listing, for that August and September, the average hourly wind-speed at all 120 U.S. weather stations.

The brothers remembered that reporters had rushed to the Indiana Dunes the day after Chanute's first successful flights, producing news stories all across the country. They wanted no such publicity.

REPORTERS BECAME THE PRESS

When the Wrights were young, television, radio, and news magazines had not yet been invented. Radio stations began broadcasting in the 1920s, and the first news magazine, *Time*, was founded in 1923. Television did not become common across the United States until the autumn of 1950.

People in the 1890s got the news by reading newspapers. Every small town had at least one weekly paper, and in every city readers could choose from several daily papers. Most cities had morning papers and evening papers, so readers could get the latest news before going to work and again after work.

Competition among newspapers was fierce. Reporters and their work had become known as "the press," a term that stemmed from the printing press. Still in use today, that phrase now includes all television, radio, newspapers, and news magazines.

The five areas with the highest winds were near cities. But the sixth-highest average wind speed in the United States was 13.4 miles (21.6 km) per hour. It was at a place few people knew anything about called Kitty Hawk, North Carolina. Autumn days there, the records showed, were usually clear and rain-free, with wind sometimes well above the average speed. That was good news, for the bicycle shop was least busy from September to December.

This photograph shows the brothers' first tent on the wind-swept dunes at Kitty Hawk. Later they built large wooden shacks in which to live and assemble their flying machines.

FIVE

WHY KITTY HAWK?

The brothers decided to ask Octave Chanute, whom they had never met, for advice. In May 1900, Wilbur wrote the first of what would become two hundred letters between the Wrights and Chanute. The reply suggested the coast of the Carolinas for its sand hills and steady winds.

TAKE APART AND PACK UP

In August, Wilbur and Orville built their glider. To make the wings' ribs, they steamed ash wood, bending it to the camber they wanted. They covered the wings with French sateen, cutting and sewing it using their sister's sewing machine so the texture ran diagonally to add strength. They designed the wing coverings so the 18-foot-long (5.5 m) spars—the leading and trailing edges—could be slipped in from the ends. The entire glider was designed to come apart and pack in a crate for shipment, and its materials cost $15. In the crate, they also packed a large tent and the tools needed to assemble their glider.

In the meantime, Wilbur wrote to Kitty Hawk's weather bureau. The bureau's only employee showed the letter to postmaster Bill Tate, who wrote, "You would find here nearly any type of ground you could wish; you could get a stretch of sandy land one mile by five with a bare hill in the center 80 feet high, not a tree or bush anywhere to break the wind. I will take pleasure in doing all I can for your convenience & success & pleasure, & I assure you you will find a hospitable people when you come among us."

All this time, Bishop Wright was on one of his lengthy trips. Katharine wrote him, "We are in an uproar getting Will off. The trip will do him good. I don't think he will be reckless. Orv will go down as soon as Will gets the machine ready."

Amid the uproar, Wilbur's thoughtful sister slipped a small jar of jam into her brother's bag. She also agreed to manage the bicycle shop, along with their brother Lorin, while Wilbur and Orville were away.

SAILING AND BAILING

Early in September, Wilbur boarded a train for Virginia. He stopped in Norfolk, expecting to buy 18-foot (5.5-m) lengths of spruce for the wing spars, but had to settle for 16-foot (4.9-m) white pine. That meant he would have to make the wings shorter, and they would have less square footage. That, in turn, meant they would not get their needed lift in a 12-mile (19.3-km)-per-hour wind but would require at least 15 miles (24.1 km) per hour.

Hunting in lumberyards for the 18-foot (5.5 m) lengths took most of a 100-degree-Fahrenheit (38° C) day. Like all properly dressed businessmen in the 1890s, Wilbur was wearing his heavy woolen suit, necktie, high starched collar, and hat. At that time, lightweight summer clothing was unknown except in truly tropical climates, and no man or woman appeared outdoors, in summer or winter, without a hat. Wilbur nearly swooned in the humid Norfolk heat.

Next, Wilbur rode a train to Elizabeth City, 35 miles (56.3 km) from Kitty Hawk. He could travel the remaining distance only by boat, but no one at the Elizabeth City docks had heard of Kitty Hawk. It took from Saturday until Tuesday before he found Israel Perry, who had a flat-bottomed fishing schooner and was willing to sail him, with his 16-foot (4.9 m) spars, heavy trunk, and suitcase, to Kitty Hawk. "The sails were rotten," Wilbur later noted, "the rope badly worn and the rudder-post half rotted off, and the cabin so dirty and vermin-infested that I kept out of it from first to last."

They sailed overnight in high winds and rough seas. The schooner leaked. Wilbur, Perry, and Perry's only shipmate had to keep bailing—scooping up the water that leaked in and tossing it overboard—almost constantly. They remained anchored for most of the next day while

READY-TO-WEAR VERSUS HANDMADE

Although the sewing machine had been invented by Elias Howe in 1846, about 80 percent of all men's suits were still made by hand in 1860. By 1890, half of all men's clothing was ready-to-wear, or made in standard sizes in large factories. Housewives, however, still made most of their own and their children's clothing. Ready-to-wear dresses for women did not appear in stores until about 1910.

Perry made repairs to the boat, then sailed on, arriving at Kitty Hawk at 9:00 P.M. For more than twenty-four hours, Wilbur had refused to eat anything offered by Perry, who was as grime-encrusted as his vermin-infested boat. Instead, Wilbur dined on the jar of jam he found in his bag.

The next morning, Bill and Addie Tate and their three daughters made Wilbur welcome, inviting him to board with them until his brother arrived with camping equipment. Addie cooked ham and eggs for the well-dressed visitor, who had eaten nothing but jam for two days.

Wilbur had noticed the shallow, open well near their door. Thinking about typhoid fever, he asked Addie to provide a pitcher of boiled water for him every morning.

The once-a-week freight boat from Elizabeth City brought the crated materials Wilbur had shipped. He assembled them, borrowing Mrs. Tate's sewing machine to reshape the wing fabric to fit the shorter wings.

HOME OF THE LOST COLONY AND BLACKBEARD

In 1900, Kitty Hawk was a few houses and stores halfway down "The Outer Banks," a line of islands and sand dunes off North Carolina's coast. No bridges or roads reached it. America's first English colony—known as "The Lost Colony" ever since it simply disappeared after 1590—was once on nearby Roanoke Island. Until he died in 1718, a pirate named Blackbeard preyed on ships stranded on the Outer Banks' dangerous shoals.

Orville got to Kitty Hawk on September 28, bringing sugar, tea, coffee, blankets, canvas cots, a bicycle's gas lamp, and other supplies.

GLIDING DOWN KILL DEVIL HILLS

For six weeks, for three to four hours a day, the brothers tested their human-carrying glider with no one aboard. They kept careful records, measuring wind speed with a hand-held instrument called an anemometer. They also measured drag, or total air resistance, with a spring from a scale usually used to weigh fish.

Finally, on October 20, they took the glider to high dunes called Kill Devil Hills. In turn, Wilbur and Orville each stretched flat and rode it in winds of 12 to 14 miles (19.3 to 22.5 km) per hour, gliding as far as 400 feet (121.9 m) in fifteen to twenty seconds. After a dozen such rides, they were pleased, for their times and distances were as good as any recorded by Lilienthal or Chanute.

The brothers test the man-sized glider at Kitty Hawk in October 1900. They spent six weeks making sure it really flew before either of them got aboard.

The brothers packed to go home. Departing, they told Bill Tate he could take the machine apart and use the materials. From the sateen wing fabric, Addie was delighted to make dresses for Irene and Pauline, who were three and four years old.

The Wright brothers had learned that they had to have much larger wings to get the lift they needed. So in the winter of 1900-1901 they designed a new glider, building wings 22 feet (6.7 m) across and 7 feet (2.1 m) from leading edge to trailing edge. They also made the camber twice as high as before.

Eager to try the new design, Wilbur and Orville hired an old friend, Charlie Taylor, who was an able bicycle mechanic. Under Katharine's supervision, he would run the shop in its busiest season—July and August—while they returned to Kitty Hawk. From there, Orville wrote to his sister that "mosquitoes came in a mighty cloud, almost darkening the sun. The sand and grass and trees and hills and everything were crawling with them. They chewed us clean through our underwear and socks. Lumps began swelling up all over my body like hen's eggs."

The bigger glider did not work as well as the previous year's had. Wilbur made many glides, but found he had poor control of pitch and roll. Often,

HOW DID THEY PAY FOR ALL THIS?

A typical worker in 1900 earned $440 a year, or $8.50 a week. The Wright Cycle shop made a good profit—$2,000 to $3,000—each year between 1896 and 1900. The brothers spent less than $300 building the 1900 and 1901 gliders, including the expenses of the two trips to Kitty Hawk.

as the nose went up too high, he stopped dead in the air 20 feet (6.1 m) above the sand and then dropped like a pancake without hurting himself or the machine. Finally he and Orville rebuilt the wings, changing the camber. Then, with pitch better controlled, he glided as far as 389 feet (118.6 m). The brothers could not understand why the wing-warping was not controlling roll as it should.

On August 22, 1901, they considered their experiments a failure and headed for home earlier than planned. On the train, Wilbur told his brother, "Not within a thousand years would man ever fly."

No sooner did the brothers reach home than Octave Chanute invited Wilbur to Chicago to make a speech to the Western Society of Engineers. Wilbur was hesitant about discussing the experiments. Katharine goaded him into saying yes, and insisted he borrow Orville's best shirt, collar, cuffs, cufflinks, and topcoat, for Orville was always better dressed. "You never saw Will look so swell," she wrote to Bishop Wright, who was out west on church business.

Wilbur described the Kitty Hawk experiments to the society's seventy members, showing them designs and pictures. He explained how roll still had to be controlled, saying "all other difficulties are of minor importance." The speech was printed in the members' magazine.

TEST PROVES LILIENTHAL WRONG

Lilienthal, Langley, and others had created tables—groupings of data in rows and columns—that showed how much lift and how much drag could be expected of various airfoils at various wind speeds. Wilbur and Orville had used Lilienthal's tables, but now they questioned them.

The brothers mounted a bicycle wheel horizontally on a hub, so it could spin easily, in front of a bike's handlebars. On one side of the wheel they attached a miniature airfoil shaped to Lilienthal's camber. One-quarter of the way around, they mounted a flat panel without camber. Pumping hard, they raced the bicycle up and down the street to see which—Lilienthal's cambered airfoil or the flat panel—best used the wind to make the wheel spin. They knew it would turn in one direction if the airfoil had the strongest lift, but would turn the opposite way if the flat panel worked better. The flat panel won, proving that Lilienthal's tables had been created through guesswork.

That led the brothers to build a wind tunnel. They made a wooden box 6 feet (182.8 cm) long and 16 by 16 inches (40.6 by 40.6 cm) wide, with a fan turning at four thousand revolutions per minute to produce a steady wind of 27 miles (43.4 km) per hour. In it they mounted airfoil

This photo is of a replica of the Wright wind tunnel that is exhibited in the Wright Cycle shop in Greenfield Village, Michigan. In their tunnel, the brothers tested about 150 airfoil designs, learning more and more about lift and drag and air pressure.

designs—several shapes and sizes—so they could discover which had the best lift.

By December of 1901, they were certain that Lilienthal's wing had been highly inefficient. They were confident that they had found the airfoil shape, with the peak of its arch only one-quarter of the distance back from the leading edge, that would enable them to fly with power.

Over the spring and summer, they built an entirely new glider with wings 10 feet (3 m) longer than before, but 2 feet (9.36 cm) narrower from leading edge to trailing edge.

ORVILLE CRASHES

Again at Kitty Hawk at the end of August 1902, Wilbur and Orville took turns making seventy-five glides in one day. On the last flight, the craft

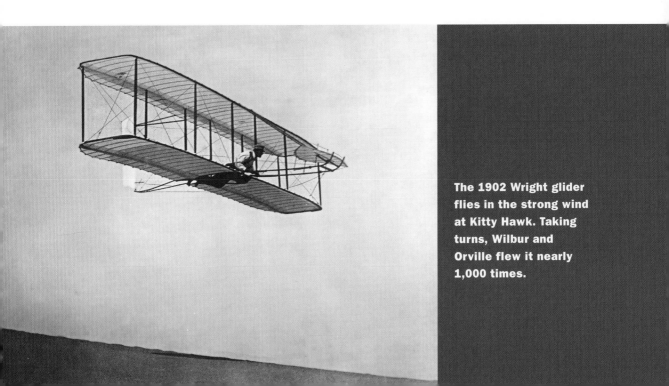

The 1902 Wright glider flies in the strong wind at Kitty Hawk. Taking turns, Wilbur and Orville flew it nearly 1,000 times.

rolled to one side and seemed to skid. As Orville tried to correct it, the nose pitched upward and the machine stalled, dropping backward onto the sand. The effect, Orville noted in his diary, was "flying machine, cloth, and sticks in a heap, with me in the center without a scratch or bruise."

In a week, they had the machine rebuilt and were gliding as far as 500 feet (152.4 m), but Orville thought about controlling that skid to the side. Lying awake, he wondered: Couldn't the rudder, which was fixed in place, offset the skidding if it could be turned left or right?

Wilbur agreed, but thought the pilot had enough to do without adding another control. They decided to make the rudder movable, but connect it to the wing-warping control so it would turn automatically. By October 10, they had the movable rudder working. That ended the skidding.

Before they left Kitty Hawk on October 28, the brothers were making flights twice as long as a football field. They knew they could control their flying machine's direction. Now they faced a final challenge: they needed to get it to take off from a standstill on level ground.

Again Wilbur and Orville put their math skills to work. They figured that wings totaling 520 square feet (48.4 sq. m) could lift 625 pounds (283.8 kg). They knew a machine that big would weigh 290 pounds (131.6 kg), not counting pilot, engine, and propellers. Either brother weighed 140 pounds (63.6 kg). So 290 plus 140 came to 430, leaving less than 200 pounds (90.8 kg) for engine and propeller. They also calculated that it would take an eight- to nine-horsepower engine to move the machine fast enough to take off.

HAD TO BUILD IT THEMSELVES

Wilbur wrote to ten makers of gasoline engines. None wanted to make one that weighed only 180 pounds (81.7 kg), yet produced nine horsepower, so within six weeks, Orville and Charlie Taylor, the bicycle machinist, built their own. "We didn't make any drawings," Taylor said later. "One of us would sketch out the part we were talking about on a piece of scratch paper and I'd tack the sketch over my bench." For the engine block, he started with a large chunk of aluminum (for its light weight), boring four cylinder holes in it. He himself made cast-iron pistons and shaped the crankshaft from a block of machine steel. The engine weighed just 19 pounds (41.9 kg) and, said Charlie, "She balanced up perfectly, too."

The engine ran with no vibration—that was important because any roughness could break the chains turning the propellers—and worked even better than expected, producing twelve horsepower.

The Wright brothers first thought they would adapt the shapes of ships' propellers for their airplane, but they soon realized that an air propeller had to have camber, like a wing, to create the thrust to pull the machine forward. Using the tables they made when researching their wing design, they created their own propellers. Each was 8.5 feet (2.6 m) long and made of three layers of spruce glued together and shaped with carpenter's tools to form the needed camber. They were pleased to find they produced an efficiency of 66 percent. That meant that 66 percent of the horsepower turning the propellers was becoming thrust—just the percentage they had hoped for.

Wilbur and Orville wanted to protect the ideas—the wing-warping and movable rudder—built into their 1902 glider. So in March of 1903,

THE PATENT OFFICE
AND FLYING MACHINES

By the 1890s, the U.S. Patent Office had received so many applications for flying-machine patents that it automatically dismissed any application unless the inventor could prove actual flight. A patent is a government document giving the inventor of a device or process the sole right to make, use, or sell the invention for a certain length of time.

they applied for a patent. The U.S. Patent Office refused, saying their machine was "incapable of performing its intended function."

While the Wrights were building their engine and shaping their propellers, Octave Chanute was in Paris, France. There, in April of 1903, he spoke before the Aero-Club de France, a group that dreamed of flying machines but had not done much about inventing them. Describing the Wright brothers' progress, Chanute stirred the club members' interest. They began organizing gliding competitions and raising prize money to encourage would-be flyers to experiment.

SIX

DECEMBER 17, 1903

By the summer of 1903, Wilbur and Orville had a new machine ready to test at Kitty Hawk. It weighed 675 pounds (306.4 kg)—more than the 625 pounds (283.7 kg) they planned—but the engine's twelve horsepower would make the wings provide the needed lift.

For takeoff, they used 2-inch (5.1-cm) by 4-inch (10.2-cm) lumber to build a 60-foot (18.3 m) track as wide as the hub of a bicycle wheel. They attached one hub to the front of the machine, and another to a small block of wood that propped up the plane's tail and would drop off when the machine lifted into the air. In effect, the hubs were rollers.

The brothers reached Kitty Hawk on September 26. They found their old camp building had been blown off its foundation by violent winter winds. They had purposely left their 1902 glider in it, for they had no reason to ship it back to Dayton. Luckily, the glider was unharmed. They used it their first day to make seventy-five glides, getting back their "feel" for gliding.

With lumber they had sent ahead, they built a new shed—44 feet (13.4 m) long, 16 feet (4.9 m) wide, and with walls 9 feet (2.7 m) high—in which to assemble their flying machine. While they worked on it, a violent four-day storm washed high tides under their floorboards, and in the wind-driven rain, Orville climbed onto the roof to nail down flapping tar paper. As the wind whipped Orville's overcoat over his back and head, Wilbur climbed up and held the coat down while Orville, his nail supply in his mouth, hammered away.

WOULD LANGLEY BEAT THEM?

Assembling the machine and engine took most of October. In the meantime, the mail brought them a newspaper clipping describing Samuel Langley's attempts to fly.

The world's first airplane hangar, built by the Wright brothers at Kitty Hawk.

Wilbur and Orville knew that Langley had spent five years building his "Great Aerodrome," a full-sized copy of his model. They also knew that the U.S. Army was paying $50,000 for the project. If Langley's plane flew before theirs did, all of their time and effort would be wasted.

The news clipping told how the Great Aerodrome, launched on October 7 from atop a houseboat on the Potomac River near Quantico, Virginia, had dropped directly into the water, nearly drowning its pilot. The article also said Langley blamed the launching system, not the aircraft, for the failure.

Next, a letter from Octave Chanute told them that Langley was planning another attempt before winter came. Hurrying to get their plane ready, they were frustrated by more storms that kept them repairing their shed instead of building the plane. On Sunday, November 1, Orville wrote to Katharine:

About a week ago the weather turned very cold (about zero according to my backbone) and another rain set in which continued for several days. We found that fire was absolutely necessary. We took one of the carbide cans and, after punching holes in the bottom for air, built a fire

The Great Aerodrome sinks in the Potomac River. Witnesses said the engine of its launching catapult somehow got turned off just as the airplane's engine was started.

in it inside the building. Of course the smoke was so intense that there was no standing up in the room, so we sat down on the floor about the can with tears streaming down our cheeks enjoying its kindly heat. Everything was sooted up so thoroughly that for several days we couldn't eat without a whole lot of black soot dropping in our plates.

DELAYED BY THE SHAKES

Five days later, the machine was ready, but the engine vibrated severely, damaging both propeller shafts. They sent them to Dayton for Charlie Taylor to repair. While waiting, they watched their stock of canned food dwindle. "We had to come down to condensed milk and crackers," Orville wrote his sister, "with coffee and rice cakes for breakfast."

When they got the shafts back, the engine still ran rough, shaking the entire machine, because the sprockets (the toothed gears that the drive chains caught hold of) would not stay tight on the shafts. Orville was thankful his tool kit included Arnstein's Cement, which Wright Cycle used to bind tires to rims. It solved the problem.

For a week, they tested the engine. Then a careful inspection revealed a crack in one propeller shaft. This time, Orville took the shafts to Dayton himself, replacing shafts of hollow tubing with shafts of solid spring steel.

He returned on December 11 with news of Langley's "Great Aerodrome." Launched again from the houseboat, it had flipped over backward. This time the pilot nearly drowned twice: first under the wreckage, then under an ice cake. Altogether, reports said, Langley's failures had cost $73,000. Orville counted up everything he and Wilbur had spent on their new machine, including travel costs. The total was less than $1,000.

With solid steel propeller shafts, the engine ran perfectly. Unfortunately, for three days Kitty Hawk had almost no wind, and the brothers sat in their shack reading. Then, on December 14, the wind picked up. From nearly a mile away, men at the U.S. Lifesaving Service Station saw a big red flag on the Wright shack. It told them the brothers were ready to try a flight. Five men and several boys hurried to help move the 700-pound (317.8 kg) machine and its 60-foot (18.3 m) track to a slope of the Kill Devil Hills dunes.

THE SOURCE OF MANY JOKES

By the time *The Washington Post* reported on October 8 that Langley's Aerodrome "simply slid into the water," newspapers everywhere were poking fun at the idea of a flying machine carrying anybody into the air. Langley's efforts were described as a "fiasco" and "complete failure."

After forty minutes' work, the plane was on its track. As the engine started, its loud chattering drove the boys away. Wilbur and Orville tossed a coin to see who would take the controls. Wilbur won.

The plane rolled down the track faster than expected, its nose pitching upward. Then it slowed, its left wingtip catching the dune, spinning the machine around and cracking one of the braces supporting the front elevator.

Repairs took two days. In the meantime, Wilbur and Orville reasoned that the launch downhill was not only too fast, but would hurt their claim that the machine flew only by its own power. So on the morning of December 17, with the help of three men from the Lifesaving Service, they positioned their launch track on level sand near their shack.

While the engine warmed up, the brothers stepped off to the side. As one of the lifesavers later said, "We couldn't help notice how they held on to each other's hand, sort o' like two folks parting who weren't sure they'd ever see one another again."

WHOSE TURN IS IT?

It was Orville's turn. He had placed his big box camera on its tripod, aiming at the end of the track. As he stretched out flat on the flying machine, his brother asked lifesaver John T. Daniels to be ready to snap the camera shutter. Then he hurried to the right wingtip and removed a small bench on which it rested. He held the wingtip as Orville moved the engine control from its center notch, for idling or warm-up speed, to a left notch for flying speed. That started a stopwatch, the wind-speed anemometer, and the propeller's revolutions per minute counter.

PATROLLING BEACHES, RESCUING SAILORS

The U.S. Lifesaving Service was established in 1871. Its employees lived along the Atlantic and Pacific coasts, patrolling beaches on foot to search for and rescue sailors whose ships, in rough weather, had run aground on dangerous reefs and shoals. In 1915, as beach patrols were no longer needed because navigation aids had improved and powerful engines had replaced sails, the service became the U.S. Coast Guard.

Slowly, the flying machine moved into a wind blowing 27 miles (43.4 km) an hour. At 40 feet (12.2 m) down the track, it rose into the air as Daniels snapped one of the world's most famous photographs. It caught Wilbur standing solidly by his brother as Orville flew their invention into history.

The airplane went just 120 feet (36.6 m) in twelve seconds. The excited group of men carried the machine back to the starting point. Now

This is one of the world's most reproduced photographs. The plate-glass negative of this image later survived a flood 8 feet deep at the Wright home at 7 Hawthorn Street in Dayton, Ohio.

ORVILLE'S CAMERA

In 1903, a serious photographer like Orville Wright still used a large box camera that had to be mounted on a tripod and that made negatives on glass plates. The box Brownie, a simple, low-cost camera that used roll film, had been introduced by George Eastman's Kodak Company only in 1900. Its easy use started the idea that anybody—and everybody—could take snapshots.

Wilbur flew 195 feet (59.4 m). Then Orville flew 200 feet (61 m). And then Wilbur flew 852 feet (259.6 m) in fifty-nine seconds.

The willing volunteers lugged the heavy machine back from that long flight. Then, a gust of wind flipped a wingtip into the air. John Daniels leapt up, grabbing a strut. The wind swept the machine over backward. It went tumbling end over end, with the engine breaking loose, Daniels screaming, struts splintering, and wires pinging as they snapped apart.

Daniels was not hurt, but the plane was a wreck. One of the helpers, Johnny Moore, raced toward Kitty Hawk to spread the news. Meeting postmaster Bill Tate, Moore shouted, "They done it! They done it! Damn'd if they ain't flew!"

SEVEN

ABOVE THE
COW PASTURE

At home in Dayton at dinnertime on December 17, 1903, Katharine and her father received a telegram:

Success four flights thursday morning all against twenty one mile wind started from Level with engine power alone average speed through air thirty one miles longest 57 seconds inform Press home Christmas.

—OREVELLE WRIGHT

The telegraph operator had both the time and Orville's name wrong (fifty-nine seconds was correct).

Katharine took the telegram, along with a press release her father had prepared days earlier, to her brother Lorin's nearby home. Lorin went that evening to *The Dayton Journal*. There reporter Frank Tunison laughed at him. "Fifty-seven seconds, hey?" he said. "If it had been fifty-seven minutes then it might have been a news item."

In Norfolk, Virginia, however, a telegraph operator who had forwarded Orville's message told a friend who told a reporter. Next morning, the *Virginian-Pilot*'s front page announced a fanciful story. The flying machine took the Wright brothers 3 miles (4.8 km), according to the newspaper article. It also said they flew 60 feet (18.3 m) high with a "huge fan-shaped rudder of canvas" that moved both side to side and up and down and that the engine hung below their "navigator's car."

Other newspapers copied the story. On their train ride home, Wilbur and Orville read the absurd reports. From Huntington, West Virginia, they

SPEEDY MESSAGES, THANKS TO MORSE

Invented in 1876, the telephone was not yet in common use in 1903. Urgent long-distance messages were sent by telegraph, and a message sent by telegraph was called a telegram. A telegraph operator tapped out a telegram letter by letter using a key, or button, that controlled electrical impulses sent through telegraph wires. This device was developed by Samuel F. B. Morse in 1836. Each letter of the alphabet was represented by dots and dashes in the Morse code, also devised by Morse.

By 1851, more than 50 telegraph companies were operating in the United States. Businesses as well as individuals used telegrams to send messages quickly. As newspapers competed with each other, they found the telegraph system especially useful for gathering urgent news.

telegraphed Katharine on December 23: "Have survived perilous trip reported in papers. Home tonight."

TRYING AND CRASHING ALL YEAR LONG

Wilbur and Orville knew they still had a lot of work to do. Their machine could lift itself off the ground, but fifty-nine seconds in the air hardly made it something that would revolutionize travel. They started building stronger engines. They got permission to use a 100-acre (40.5-hectare) meadow near Dayton called Huffman Prairie and on it built a shed in which they could assemble their next airplane.

This is the absurd headline and imaginative story published by the *Virginian-Pilot* the day after the first flight. Without hesitation, other newspapers copied the story.

During 1904, they worked at improving the machine and their control of it, shattering wings and smashing propellers in countless tries and crashes. Not until August did they fly farther than their 852-foot (259.6 m) Kitty Hawk record. Then, on September 20, in one minute and thirty-five seconds, Orville flew all the way around the field—some 4,080 feet (1,244.4 m). By December 9, each brother could circle the field four or five times, flying for as long as five minutes.

That fall, a British army officer visited Wilbur and Orville. English military men, he said, had Octave Chanute's reports on the Wrights' success and could foresee winning wars by controlling the air. He urged them to sell their airplane to the British War Office.

Wilbur wrote to Chanute, "We would be ashamed if we offered our machine to a foreign government without giving our own country a chance at it." However, the U.S. Army refused to consider their machine. After all, the army had spent $50,000 on the worthless Langley Aerodrome.

In the spring of 1905, Wilbur and Orville kept trying to improve their machine and kept having minor crashes. Then a severe crash at 30 miles (48.3

Orville and Wilbur (left to right) and the Wright Flyer at Huffman Prairie in May 1904. The effect of wing-warping can be seen in the bent-looking shapes of the upper and lower wings.

km) per hour on July 14 smashed the plane, leaving Orville bruised and dazed. That made them rethink its basic design. They made the front elevator a third larger and extended it more than 4 feet (1.2 m) farther out front. The change ended the crashes, and by September, much longer flights were common. Wilbur flew for more than eighteen minutes—until the gas tank emptied—on September 26, and then more than thirty-three minutes on October 4.

The next day, as a small crowd of neighbors and friends watched, Wilbur circled the field for more than thirty-nine minutes, covering more than 24 miles (38.6 km) as he again emptied the tank. "The durned thing just kept going round," said farmer Amos Stauffer. "I thought it would never stop." What Stauffer had seen was the world's first practical airplane.

A YEAR WITHOUT FLYING

Newspaper reporters heard about that flight and hurried to Huffman Prairie. But the brothers still had no patent, so they didn't want anyone telling the world how their machine worked. They decided to make no

A replica of the 1905 hangar at Huffman Prairie as it appears today at Wright-Patterson Air Force Base.

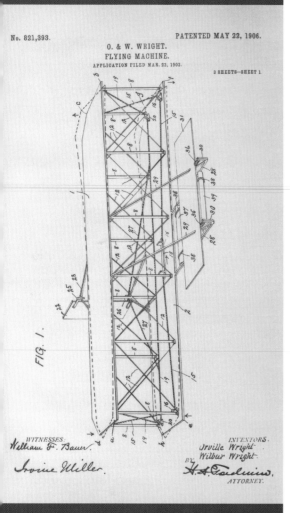

No. 821,393.

PATENTED MAY 22, 1906.

O. & W. WRIGHT.
FLYING MACHINE.
APPLICATION FILED MAR. 23, 1903.

3 SHEETS—SHEET 1.

FIG. 1.

WITNESSES:
William F. Bauer.

Jouie Miller.

INVENTORS.
Orville Wright
Wilbur Wright
BY
H. A. Toulmin.
ATTORNEY.

The patent issued on May 22, 1906. Note that, while Wilbur's name usually came first on everything, the bureaucratic Patent Office identified the patent holders in alphabetical order as "O. & W. WRIGHT."

more flights until they had their patent and a contract for the purchase of their invention.

Both the U.S. Army and the British War Office demanded detailed descriptions and demonstrations before they would consider buying the Wright Flyer. The brothers refused, insisting on agreements in advance.

They tried France, where inventors were eager to fly. The French government made a $5,000 deposit on the Wrights' price of $200,000, but then backed off, leaving the deposit with the brothers.

Meanwhile, Wilbur and Orville quietly accepted such comments as appeared in the Paris edition of *The New York Herald Tribune* on February 10, 1906: "The Wrights have flown or they have not flown. They possess a machine or they do not possess one. They are in fact either fliers or liars. It is difficult to fly. It is easy to say, 'We have flown.'"

On May 22, 1906, the United States issued patent No. 821,393 for the Wright Flying Machine. By then, patent applications had been approved in Belgium, France, and Great Britain, and approvals from Italy, Germany, and Austria came later that year. "Isn't it astonishing," Orville wrote to his friend George Spratt, "that all of these secrets have been preserved for so many years just so that we could discover them!"

SILVER TROPHY FOR TWENTY-ONE-SECOND FLIGHT

Others kept trying to discover the secrets. In France, the Aero-Club offered a silver trophy to anyone who first flew a motorized plane 80 feet (24.4 m). In Paris in November of 1906, more than a year after Wilbur Wright had flown 24 miles (38.6 km), a Brazilian named Alberto Santos-Dumont was acclaimed a hero when he won the trophy by flying only 722 feet (220.2 m) in twenty-one seconds.

American headlines called Santos-Dumont's flight "The First Important Demonstration of an Aeroplane in Public," and the secretary of the Aero Club of America said it "marks the most positive advance yet made in the science of aeronautics."

"There is absolutely no evidence to support the alleged statements of the Wright brothers," Santos-Dumont told reporters. "They may have flown, but nothing in any report of their proceedings inspires confidence."

None of that bothered the Wright brothers. They, and the dozens of Daytonians who had watched them at Huffman Prairie, knew what they had done. They waited.

SAYING NO

A letter came to the Wrights in May 1906 from Glenn Curtiss, whose company built five hundred motorcycles a year. Wouldn't his lightweight engines be useful in flying machines? he asked. Curtiss visited Dayton and met the brothers, who showed him photographs of their earlier machines in flight. They did not let him see the plane itself.

In November, a proposal came from a well-known American business-man named Charles Flint. An investment banker, he had organized many giant corporations and had sold fleets of American ships to Brazil, Chile, Russia, and Japan.

Flint offered to buy all foreign rights to the Wright Flyer for $500,000. That would leave the brothers free to sell the plane to U.S. buyers at any price. They said no. Next, Flint offered to be their agent overseas, splitting all profits fifty-fifty after the Wrights earned the first $50,000. Again they refused.

In May of 1907, the president of the Aero Club of America got a con-gressman to tell President Theodore Roosevelt about the brothers' feats. Roosevelt alerted Secretary of War William Howard Taft, who stirred the army's interest, but it asked for exclusive rights to the airplane. The brothers refused.

Meanwhile, Flint urged the Wrights to go to Europe and meet his agent, Hart O. Berg, for talks with possible buyers. Wilbur sailed from New York on May 18.

In France, Berg—who had at first doubted that two bicycle makers could create much of an airplane—became a staunch supporter of the brothers. He began negotiating with the French government. Between meetings, Wilbur took in the sights of Paris, but was disappointed. He wrote Katharine that the *Mona Lisa* was "no better than the prints in black and white." And Notre Dame cathedral? He preferred Victor Hugo's description in *The Hunchback of Notre Dame*. "The nave," he wrote, "is seemingly not much wider than a storeroom." He added that those windows way up at the top didn't let in much light.

Wilbur also told his sister about a balloon flight he took with three other men. They rose to 3,000 feet (914.4 m) and traveled 20 miles (32.18 km), but, Wilbur wrote, "a few glorious hours in the air are usually followed by a tiresome walk to some village, an uncomfortable night at a poor hotel, and a return home by slow local trains."

At home, Orville worked on improvements to the airplane. The long 1905 flights had exhausted the pilot, who had to lie on his belly and warp the wings by moving side-to-side in a hip cradle. And both European and U.S. Armies requested that demonstration flights carry a passenger. So Orville sat them both upright with dual controls so the pilot could teach the passenger how to control the airplane.

NO CONTRACT, NO FLIGHTS

In July 1907, Orville sailed for France. With him he took one plane and Charlie Taylor so they were ready to assemble the machine and give demonstration flights, but only after signing contracts.

They came home in November having signed no contracts and made no demonstrations. They left one crated airplane in Le Havre, France. They also left the impression that they were frauds, for the French had seen Frenchman Henri Farman fly a Voisin plane for almost 53 seconds on

October 26. Then, on November 18, as Orville watched, Farman had flown a nearly complete circle. No one had seen a Wright flight in Europe.

Back home, the Wrights found that the army was seriously interested in their flyer. They set their price—one machine for $25,000—and the army set specifications. The plane had to carry pilot and passenger at a speed of 40 miles (64.3 km) per hour, flying for at least one hour. It also had to be "capable of dismounting and loading on an army wagon to be transported." Just as they had this chance at a contract with the United States, Hart Berg sent word that French financiers were ready to buy the brothers' French patents and make and sell Wright planes there.

Wilbur and Orville had not flown for two years. They decided to return to Kitty Hawk, where they could practice flying their improved machine away from snooping eyes. In December of 1907, before they went, they received a letter from Glenn Curtiss, the motorcycle builder who had visited Dayton in September of 1906. He said he had been working with Alexander Graham Bell's Aerial Experiment Association (AEA) to build an airplane powered by a lightweight engine.

Next came a letter from Thomas E. Selfridge, a West Point graduate working with the AEA. Eager to get the army into flying, he asked many questions. The Wrights' reply gave him only information protected by their patents.

REPORTERS SHOW UP AT KITTY HAWK

At Kitty Hawk in April, Wilbur and Orville found the dunes strewn with airplane wings and pieces of their camp buildings. By May 1, they had built a new hangar and assembled a plane. That day, the Norfolk *Virginian-Pilot* again invented news, saying the Wrights had just flown 10 miles (16 m) over the ocean. Soon a crowd of reporters was riding motorboats to the Outer Banks. On May 14, they saw Wilbur take Charlie Furnas, a Dayton mechanic who had traveled to Kitty Hawk on his own because he wanted to fly, on a short flight—the first ever by two people together. Later that day, Wilbur flew 8,909 feet (2.7 km), or more than 1.5 miles (2.4 km), in seven minutes.

Telegrams kept coming from Flint & Company saying the French wanted to see demonstrations. Wilbur headed for New York, telegraphing Katharine to send his bags to meet him. While Wilbur was in Europe, Orville would demonstrate the Wright Flyer for the army.

Before he sailed, Wilbur wrote a letter to thank his sister for sending his clothes, adding that he hoped next time she would "raise the lid of my

At Kitty Hawk in May 1908, newspaper reporters hide in underbrush along the dunes while waiting to see the Wright brothers fly. One report said, "Men trained to observe details under all sorts of distractions, forgot their cameras, forgot their watches, forgot everything but this aerial monster chattering over our heads."

hatbox and put some of my hats in before sending it on." He added that he could buy hats in New York.

Wilbur also wrote to Orville about a newspaper article that described the use of ailerons, which are movable wingtips on hinges, on the AEA plane. "Selfridge," he wrote, "is infringing our patent on wing twisting." Saying "a statement of our original features ought to be published," he urged Orville to write an article for *The Century* magazine describing how they created the Wright Flyer.

THE FOREMOST BIRDMEN

In Le Havre, the crated airplane parts had waited since November. Wilbur had them shipped to a field near Le Mans, 100 miles (160.9 km) from Paris. Unfortunately, when he opened them, he found that the crates held a mess of bent axles, crushed seats, and torn cloth. Enraged, Wilbur wrote his brother: "I opened the boxes yesterday, and have been puzzled ever since to know how you could have wasted two whole days packing them. I am sure that with a scoop shovel I could have put things in within two or three minutes and made fully as good a job of it. I never saw such evidence of idiocy in my life."

Orville, who could tell that his brother's patience was stretched thin, did not protest his innocence, but guessed what had happened: French customs inspectors had examined the contents of the crates and then failed to repack them carefully.

Wilbur spent six weeks making repairs and assembling his plane. Meanwhile, on the Fourth of July at Hammondsport, New York, Glenn Curtiss flew 5,360 feet (1,633 km) in one minute and forty seconds, winning a $2,500 silver sculpture offered by the Aero Club of America. Orville read that Curtiss controlled his plane with hinged movable wingtips. He wrote to Curtiss, saying the Wright patent covered all essential elements, including movable wingtips. He and Wilbur, he concluded, "did not intend to give permission to use the patented features of our machines."

On Saturday, August 8, as a few Frenchmen watched, Wilbur took off and flew around the field twice in two minutes. The astonished spectators not only saw Wilbur Wright fly. They saw him maneuver in great sweeping curves, his wings banked deeply into each turn. No French pilot had demonstrated such control. The newspapers cheered. By Thursday, crowds hurried to Le Mans to gape as Wilbur was circling the field as many as seven times in eight minutes and thirteen seconds. Within days, Hart Berg and a local military man had to set up a ticket system to control the crowds as Wilbur again and again proved that he and his brother were, in the words of one French witness, "les premiers hommes-oiseaux"—the foremost birdmen.

FIRST DEATH IN AN AIR CRASH

Orville arrived in Fort Myer, Virginia, for his demonstrations for the army on August 20. Its contract would pay $25,000 if the Wright Flyer proved able to hold an average speed of 40 miles (64.4 m) per hour, with a bonus of $2,500 for each extra mile or kilometer per hour it flew.

Orville flew first on September 3, circling the field once. Crowds gathered. Within a week, he not only made his first public flight with a passenger, but set and broke his own records, finally flying for seventy minutes and twenty-four seconds.

Now it was time to fly a member of the army board that was judging the demonstrations. It was none other than Lieutenant Selfridge, who had worked with Glenn Curtiss on the AEA plane and had written the Wrights trying to get information on their plane.

They took off in the afternoon of September 17 and circled the field three times. Then, planning a wider turn, Orville pitched the nose upward, climbing above 100 feet (30.48 m) and heading toward Arlington Cemetery. Then he heard an unusual tapping sound.

He decided to turn back and land. Now came two loud thumps. The plane shook furiously. Orville cut off the power. The plane skidded to the right with its left wing down. The nose pitched downward. Selfridge muttered, "Oh! Oh!"

They hit the ground at full speed. Pilot and passenger, both unconscious and bleeding, were tangled in a mass of wreckage. Orville's left thigh and several ribs were broken, his scalp cut and bruised. Selfridge's skull was fractured. He died—the first fatality in an air crash—within hours.

Spectators at the crash site at Arlington Cemetery help raise the wreckage to free the unconscious Lieutenant Thomas E. Selfridge. Others, including a doctor in the crowd, tend to Orville Wright, who has already been moved from the wreckage.

AS THICK AS THIEVES

People wanted to know what caused the accident. Mechanics Taylor and Furnas soon figured out that the right-hand propeller had split along one of its layers—just enough to flatten the blade slightly. This changed its thrust so it pulled out of line and clipped one of the taut wires that kept the rudder in position. With the rudder twisted, the plane dove out of control. Army officers, understanding the explanation, told Orville that the brothers could finish their demonstrations the following summer.

Katharine rushed to the Fort Myer hospital and stayed at her brother's bedside the entire seven weeks he was there. "The nurses are nice," she wrote to a friend, "but Orville likes to see me." With Orville barely conscious at first, she added, "I kept him quiet by reading to him. The monotonous sound of my voice puts him to sleep." It was November 1 when, with Orville using crutches, they returned to Dayton.

With Wilbur Wright at the controls, Edith Berg smiles, ready to become the first woman aloft in a powered flying machine. Note Wilbur's starched wing collar and the cord tying Mrs. Berg's skirt around her ankles.

WILBUR SETS A NEW STYLE

In France, Wilbur was breaking records and amazing crowds as large as ten thousand. In October and November he flew more than forty passengers, including men from Italy, Spain, Russia, Germany, and England.

Hart Berg's wife, Edith, had the fun of being the first woman to fly. Before takeoff, Wilbur gathered her flaring skirt, tying it around her ankles so the wind couldn't whip it into the flight mechanism. Within days, fashion designers made flared skirts tight at the bottom. Soon stylish ladies on both sides of the Atlantic were wearing the popular "hobbled skirt." Wilbur also set styles for men. The soft cloth cap he wore while flying soon turned up on thousands of male French heads. It became known as the "Veelbur Reet" cap.

The excitement continued. While weather and airplane repairs kept

Wilbur on the ground for several days, a seventy-year-old man who hoped to see a flight rode his bicycle 30 miles (48 km) each way daily for almost a week.

Crowds from Paris thronged the Le Mans hotels and enriched the drivers who taxied them to the field. Bouquets of flowers and baskets of fruit kept arriving at Wilbur's shack. After he flew for an hour and a half on September 21, Wilbur was invited to speak at a spirited reception. The French learned of his wit and his dislike of public speaking when he said, "I know of only one bird, the parrot, that talks, and it can't fly very high."

Among those who hurried to fly with Wilbur at Le Mans was Major Baden Fletcher Smyth Baden-Powell, whose brother had founded the Boy Scouts. He later wrote about the airplane's ride:

So steady is the motion that it appears as if it were progressing along an invisible elevated track. Only as a swirl of wind catches it does it make a slight undulation like a boat rising to a big wave. Mr. Wright, with both hands grasping the levers, watches every move, but his movements are so slight as to be almost imperceptible. The machine is guided in a large semi-circle, gracefully leaning over as it turns. All the time the engine is buzzing so loudly and the propellers humming so that after a trip one is almost deaf.

In five months living near Le Mans, Wilbur made 129 flights. Among those who watched or flew with him, he wrote to Orville, "Princes and millionaires" appeared to be "as thick as thieves."

THREE WRIGHTS POPULAR IN EUROPE

In January of 1909, Orville and Katharine sailed for Europe. Wilbur met them in Paris. Then they moved to Pau, a resort village in the south of France. There Wilbur taught three Frenchmen how to fly, and the three Wrights were held in awe by European rulers. King Alfonso XIII of Spain took their pictures. England's King Edward VII watched as Wilbur tied a rope around Katharine's flaring skirt, as he had tied Edith Berg's, and then took her for her first flight. Lord Arthur Balfour, former prime minister of England, asked for the privilege of "taking part in the miracle" by helping to launch one flight.

Katharine Wright was good at remembering faces and names. She knew her brothers were both timid and reserved—the opposite of the kinds of salesmen they needed to be to sell their invention. She took charge of

This is a typical photo of the Wright Flyer soaring past one of its countless crowds. Note the spectators who have climbed up the launching tower to improve their view. Roped to the Flyer, a heavy weight dropped from the tower to yank the airplane into motion along its narrow launch track.

organizing their social affairs and creating the friendly atmosphere in which two bachelor geniuses could succeed, despite their shyness. And soon the European newspapers began calling her "the third Wright brother."

They went to Italy in April. Industrialist Giovanni Pirelli, whom Wilbur had flown at Le Mans, paid $10,000 for demonstrations and for the training of two pilots. Those who watched included King Victor Emmanuel and his mother, Queen Margherita, and the famed American banker J. P. Morgan.

It was time to head home. The Wrights stopped in London to arrange contracts for a British company to build six planes. While there, they learned that New York officials were planning an elaborate celebration for their arrival, with President William Howard Taft invited to present them with gold medals from the U.S. Congress, the Smithsonian Institution, and the Aero Club of America. Wilbur cabled New York that he and Orville had to go straight to Dayton to prepare for the postponed army demonstrations.

United States President William Howard Taft poses on the White House portico with Wilbur Wright to his right and Orville and Katharine to his left. Note that the brothers hold in their hands the boxes containing their medals, which have already been awarded.

AN ELABORATE CARNIVAL

Wilbur, Orville, and Katharine reached Dayton on May 13, expecting a quiet get-together with friends and family. Instead, they found ten thousand cheering people waiting for them when their train arrived. Rather than celebrating, the brothers went to work getting their aircraft ready for the Fort Myer tests.

They took time off in June to travel to Washington for the celebration. It began with a festive luncheon at the Cosmos Club. The presence of Katharine, who now accompanied her brothers at all public events and joined in all private decision-making, caused the club to break its rule against letting women enter the club. In her honor, ladies were included among the 159 guests at the luncheon.

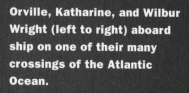

Orville, Katharine, and Wilbur Wright (left to right) aboard ship on one of their many crossings of the Atlantic Ocean.

At the White House, President Taft presented them the gold medal of the Aero Club of America. Then Taft—probably the most overweight president the United States has known—assured the brothers that, while his own size would keep him from flying, he shared everyone's interest in the subject.

Back in Dayton, the brothers faced "The Wright Brothers' Home Days Celebration" on June 17 and 18. It was not something they had looked forward to. "The Dayton presentation," Wilbur had written to Octave Chanute beforehand, "has been made the excuse for an elaborate carnival and advertisement of the city under the guise of being an honor to us. As it was done against our known wishes, we are not as appreciative as we might be."

The celebration included lively concerts, gala parades, and lengthy speeches and receptions. Schools were closed for two days, and only necessary businesses were open. Two old friends, Ed Sines and Edgar Ellis, Dayton's assistant city auditor, joined the brothers to ride in a horse-drawn carriage from the bicycle shop to the ceremonies. Along the way, Wilbur

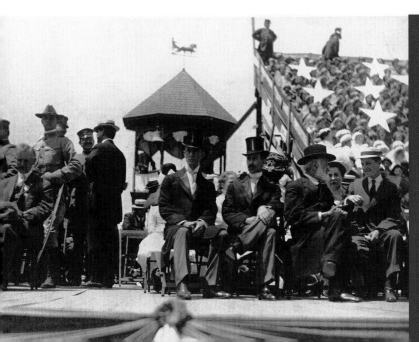

At "The Wright Brothers' Home Days Celebration," June 17 and 18, 1909, Wilbur and Orville sit front and center with their white-bearded father, Bishop Milton Wright. Note the schoolchildren massed in the grandstand as a "living flag."

and Orville sat well back and let the other men reach out to shake hands with people who thought they were greeting the famous inventors.

At one point in the opening ceremony, the printed program called for "Responses by the Wrights." Wilbur stood, said, "Thank you, gentlemen," and sat down. Several times between parades and speeches, both brothers hurried back to the bicycle shop to work on their army plane. There they hung canvas over the windows to keep the crowds on the sidewalk from watching them.

The mayor, the governor, and an army general presented gold medals while hundreds of schoolchildren wearing red, white, and blue formed a "living flag" across the giant grandstand at the fairgrounds. Wilbur and Orville each wore a tall silk hat and a formal frock coat—a coat that was usually double-breasted and hung down to the knees in the front and back. After dark, they found themselves depicted in fireworks portraits 8 feet (2.44 m) tall.

THE ONE CAR FOR EVERYBODY

Well-to-do Americans had been buying automobiles ever since the Duryea brothers, Charles and Frank, built the first gasoline-powered American car in 1893. On October 1, 1908, Henry Ford introduced the Model T, a basic automobile that, unlike the fancy, expensive cars then on the market, had no extra gadgets and accessories. It cost $850 and came in only one model and color. Ford himself is rumored to have said, "Customers can have any color they want as long as it's black." To keep costs low, Ford invented the assembly line, which became a standard system in countless factories worldwide. The Model T Ford put people everywhere on the road.

NINE

CHARMING ALL OF EUROPE AND NEW YORK

At Fort Myer, Wilbur and Orville were as cautious as ever. On June 26, 1909, with the entire U.S. Congress present by invitation from the army, they refused to fly because the wind was too strong. "Wrights Fail To Fly," said one headline, "Snub Congressmen, Brothers No Diplomats."

By the end of July, however, Orville had set a solo record of one hour and twenty minutes, a passenger record of one hour, twelve minutes, and an altitude record of 400 feet (121.9 m). He reached an average speed of 42.58 miles (68.5 km) per hour—well above the requirement. The resulting contract priced their first army plane at $30,000.

Huge crowds witnessed these demonstrations. Washington society came to Fort Myer in their expensive new automobiles and older horse-drawn carriages. Working people walked or rode trolley cars powered by electricity along city streets. Toward sundown after work, many people brought along picnic sandwiches and drinks. The daughter of former President Theodore Roosevelt, Alice Roosevelt Longworth, entertained friends by serving tea from her new electricity-powered automobile. And President Taft himself saw the speed flight that set the $30,000 price for the Wright Flyer.

While the Wrights were at Fort Myer, French flyer Louis Bleriot took off from Calais on July 26 and flew across the English Channel to Dover. The world gasped even more than it had at the Wrights. Bleriot had seen Wilbur's first public flight almost a year earlier, and since then had built several planes that used wing warping. English author H. G. Wells, who was famed for thinking ahead to future technology, informed his countrymen that "this is no longer, from a military point of view, an inaccessible island."

VISITING LAWYERS AND KAISER

Now came word that on June 26, motorcycle maker Glenn Curtiss had sold his first airplane. Wilbur went to New York and filed a legal bill of complaint to keep Curtiss from making, selling, or exhibiting airplanes. He also filed

At the Fort Myer demonstrations, Orville Wright (seen standing center, within the structure of the airplane) checks the engine of the Wright Model A Flyer as it sits on its launch rail.

WAS PEARY FIRST AT THE POLE?

On September 6, 1909, headlines told the world that Admiral Robert Edwin Peary had led a crew of five other men and forty sled dogs across the frozen Arctic Ocean. They had reached the North Pole on April 6 and believed they were the first men ever there. Five days before Peary's announcement, however, Dr. Frederick A. Cook had revealed that his own expedition had discovered the pole on April 21, 1908, almost a year before Peary got there. The two explorers were later to spend years defending their claims, but Peary was finally considered the discoverer of the North Pole.

suit to prevent the buyer of the Curtiss plane from operating it. Meanwhile, Katharine and Orville sailed for Germany, where Orville was to set up a company to sell airplanes in Germany, Turkey, Denmark, Sweden, Norway, and Luxembourg and offer demonstration flights and pilot training.

At the same time, Curtiss was in Reims, France, flying in a weeklong air show that boasted twenty-three planes of ten different types making 120 takeoffs. Seven flew circles for more than 60 miles (96.5 km) and one went 111.8 miles (179.9 km). All Wright records, including altitude and speed, were broken. At Berlin and Potsdam, Germany, between August 30 and October 4, Orville made nineteen flights before crowds as huge as 200,000, flying higher and longer than anyone had flown in Reims.

In Germany, the emperor, Kaiser Wilhelm II, welcomed Orville and Katharine and introduced them to Count von Zeppelin, the inventor of giant dirigible airships. The kaiser approved as Orville took his son, Crown Prince Frederick Wilhelm, for a fifteen-minute flight—the first taken by any royalty. Safely back on the ground, Wilhelm pulled a stickpin from his necktie. The pin was a *W* formed by diamonds and rubies. Presenting it, the prince

GRANDSON OF QUEEN VICTORIA

Kaiser, the German word for the Latin word *Caesar* (which means "emperor"), was the title used by the three emperors of modern Germany between 1861 and 1918. The third emperor, Kaiser Wilhelm II, was the grandson of England's Queen Victoria. He ruled from 1888 until after Germany was defeated in 1918, ending World War I. During his reign, the German army and navy became among the world's most powerful.

noted that the initial stood for Wright as well as for Wilhelm.

On the same day, in a twenty-minute flight, Orville climbed to a record 1,600 feet (487.7 m). And the next week, he joined members of the royal family to fly aboard a Zeppelin dirigible from Frankfurt to Mannheim. The crowd at Mannheim was so boisterous that Orville and his interpreter were separated. Orville, the guest of honor at a planned luncheon, couldn't remember where it was to be held. He wandered the streets until he was found by a member of the reception committee who had been frantically searching for him.

A MILLION NEW YORKERS CHEER

In the United States, a two-week-long celebration was to mark the one hundredth anniversary of Robert Fulton's first steamboat voyage and the three hundredth anniversary of Henry Hudson's entering New York Harbor. The Hudson-Fulton Celebration Aeronautics Committee offered Wilbur Wright $15,000 for a one-hour or 10-mile (16.1 km) flight. It offered Glenn Curtiss $5,000 for a round-trip flight from Governors Island in New York Harbor to Grant's Tomb, which is the burial place of Ulysses S. Grant, former U.S. president and Civil War general, in northern Manhattan.

Curtiss could not use his winning plane from Reims because it was already on display at Wanamaker's New York department store. He tried a flight with a less powerful plane, but decided to quit. Wilbur Wright then took off with a red canoe strapped under his Flyer in case of emergency. He flew to the Statue of Liberty and back. Five days later, on October 4, he made the 20-mile (32.2 km) round trip to Grant's Tomb that Curtiss had promised. One million New Yorkers saw some part of the flight.

A unique system was used to let people know when to watch. Among some forty U.S. and foreign ships anchored in the Hudson, many had the new Marconi wireless transmitters, the forerunner of radio broadcasting. They received messages in Morse code from Governors Island when a flight was to begin. Meanwhile, on Governors Island, the Army Signal

Interior of the General Assembly Department at the American Wright Company factory in Dayton. Note that the Flyers now have wheeled landing gear.

GENERAL ASSEMBLY DEPARTMENT

Corps hoisted flags that could be seen from Manhattan skyscrapers, which then flew their own signal flags. As a result, Wilbur flew above honking foghorns, shrieking whistles, clanging bells, and cheering crowds. When the celebration ended, however, the committee could not afford the $15,000 it had promised Wilbur. They paid him $12,500.

Then the J. P. Morgan investment banking firm created the American Wright Company to build and sell airplanes. It paid the brothers $100,000 in cash for their patents and expert advice. The brothers also received one-third of the company stock and 10 percent of the price of every plane sold.

In January of 1910, Federal Judge John R. Hazel issued an injunction, or an order from a court that requires a person to do or not to do some specific thing, keeping the Curtiss company from making, selling, or exhibiting airplanes. He said that, because hinged ailerons were the same as wing-warping, Curtiss had infringed the Wright patent. Curtiss closed his business but appealed to a higher court. Six months later, the U.S. Circuit Court of Appeals decided that there wasn't enough proof that an infringement of the Wrights' patent had occurred. Curtiss reopened his business.

The Wrights also had to bring suits against airplane companies that they found infringing their patents in France and Germany. One of the main arguments against them in Europe was that their wing-warping system had been made public before any patent was granted. Octave Chanute had described it in his speech to the Aero-Club de France in 1903, and Wilbur had detailed it in his speech to the Western Society of Engineers in 1901 in Chicago. Nevertheless, the brothers argued that they had patented the only effective way to control an airplane in flight.

TEN

PILOTS, CROWDS, AND PROFITS

Early in 1910, the Wright company began building planes in Dayton. Each one carried only the pilot and one passenger, usually a student pilot. Airplanes were so amazing to people that huge crowds would pay admission at air shows just to watch them fly. Air-show producers booked entertainers to keep crowds amused between flights, and bands played lively tunes while pilots performed above.

The Wrights decided to enter the exhibition business. They taught pilots in Montgomery, Alabama, and at Huffman Prairie. There, on May 21, Wilbur made his last flight in the United States as a pilot. On May 26, the brothers flew together for the first time, with Orville as pilot. Until then, they had not risked losing both their lives in a single accident. On the same

Famous Pilots Taught by Orville Wright

Student pilots who learned at Huffman Prairie included several who went on to careers that made headlines. Among them were Lieutenants John Rodgers and Kenneth Whiting, the first U.S. Navy pilots, and Calbraith Perry Rodgers, the first person to fly from coast to coast (it took him eighty-four days). The commandant of U.S. Army Air Forces in World War II, Henry H. "Hap" Arnold, received his first training from Orville Wright. Another alumnus of the Wright school was Roy Brown, the Canadian pilot who shot down German ace Manfred von Richthofen—the Red Baron—in World War I.

day, Orville took his father aloft. "Higher, Orville, higher," insisted the eighty-one-year-old as they circled the field for seven minutes.

Wright pilots lived under strict rules: no gambling, no drinking of alcohol, no Sunday flights. Pay was $20 a week, plus $50 a day for actual flying time. Producers of air shows paid the Wright company $1,000 for each day's flying, and many were six-day shows.

STUNTS AND CRASHES

The planes were shipped from city to city in railroad freight cars. The flying fields were makeshift—the infield of a fairground's horse racetrack or any smooth and level pasture near town. The Wright flying team's first show was at the Indianapolis Motor Speedway (already built for auto races) in June of 1910. The show's officials were disappointed when the airplanes simply flew round and round the track. "The age is one of speed and competition," said one, "and I want to see a flock of airships fighting for first place."

Competition came from Glenn Curtiss. He created his own air-show team, paying pilots more than the Wrights paid. One Curtiss pilot caught the spirit of exhibition crowds. "They thought you were a fake," he said. "There wasn't anybody who believed an airplane would really fly. But when you flew, oh my, they would carry you off the field."

Orville himself remembered long afterward how stunned people were. "Flight was generally looked upon as an impossibility," he said, "and scarcely anyone believed in it until he had actually seen it."

At Indianapolis, spectators saw Wright pilot Walter Brookins set an altitude record of 6,000 feet (1,828 m) and then, when his motor died, glide to earth. At Asbury Park, New Jersey, they watched him crash, injuring himself and spectators. While landing, he had to swerve away from photographers running onto the field. In Milwaukee, pilot Arch Hoxsey lost control while passing the grandstand, hitting the ground and injuring people who had paid to watch the show. Wilbur then wrote to his crew

At Milwaukee in 1910, the Wright flying team's Arch Hoxsey buzzes the racetrack, thrilling the packed crowd.

before a Detroit meet: "I want no stunts and spectacular frills put on the flights there. Anything beyond plain flying will be chalked up as a fault."

The pilots ignored the warning. Hoxsey and Ralph Johnstone, known as the "Stardust Twins," gave crowds what they paid for: stunts such as The Dive of Death, in which they flew to 1,000 feet (304.8 m), dove straight down, and leveled off at the last moment.

FLYING BACKWARDS

The crowd got an unexpected sight in October at the United States's first international air meet at the Belmont Park racetrack on Long Island, New York. Johnstone and Hoxsey announced they would try, in separate planes, for new altitude records. But at 1,000 feet (304.8 m), a commanding west wind took charge. Spectators gasped as the planes, headed west with their engines at highest power, "flew" backwards out of sight to the east. The trips took Hoxsey 25 miles (40.2 km) and Johnstone 55 miles (88.5 km) before they managed to land.

In Denver in November, Johnstone became the first professional pilot to die in a crash in the United States. On the opening day of the show, he had circled the field at 1,500 feet (457.2 m) with Brookins criss-crossing below at 1,000 feet (304.8 m), while Hoxsey did figure-eights between them. The next day, with the grandstand band playing merrily, Johnstone climbed to 800 feet (243.8 m), banked over into the spiraling dive he was known for, and never recovered. As the band still played, the crowd surged onto the field to pick souvenirs, including the gloves from the dead pilot's hands, from the wreckage.

A month later, a spiral dive and crash killed Hoxsey. Wilbur thought he fell out of his plane. No one had invented the seat belt yet, and more than one pilot or passenger in those years died from simply falling out of the plane during flight maneuvers.

At the Wright school, Orville's inventive mind created the first flight simulator. It was an outdated airplane mounted on sawhorses so it could tip from side to side. A motorized belt moved it so the student had to work the controls to keep it level. Students "flew" the simulator for several days before taking off in the real thing.

In November of 1911, the brothers quit the exhibition business, saying they wanted more time for experimental work. In 1910 alone, the Wright Company had made a $100,000 profit, half of which was theirs. Since there was no income tax at that time, they didn't have to pay taxes on their earnings. Longtime Wright mechanic Charlie Taylor earned $1,300 that year. At that time, typical annual earnings for a factory worker were from $600 to $800.

ELEVEN

PROTECTED BY LAW AND MUD

Wilbur spent March to August of 1911 in Europe. In France, Germany, and England, he found that companies he and Orville had licensed to build planes could not make motors that worked well, nor could they manage simple business practices such as bookkeeping. In the courtroom, however, he won eleven suits for patent infringement against Frenchmen who claimed they had used wing warping before the Wrights patented it.

Wilbur wrote to Katharine about one English pilot who rebuilt his plane and "added porches, attics and sheds till it looks like a farm house which has been in the family for generations. When he jams a wing into the ground and whirls around, he says he can turn quicker that way than any other."

Back in the United States, Orville's nimble brain was refining an idea that he and Wilbur had first tried to patent in 1908: an automatic control so the pilot didn't have to keep making adjustments. It used a pendulum and a vane that sensed changes in position in the air and triggered compressed-air cylinders to move the elevator and warp the wings.

In October, Orville went to Kitty Hawk to test his automatic pilot where newsmen wouldn't see him. However, six reporters arrived and he decided not to let the world know about the invention until it was patented. Instead, he spent two weeks gliding in the steady wind. On October 24, 1911, he set a record that would stand for ten years. His powerless glider hung in the air for nine minutes, forty-five seconds, doing what is known today as "soaring." In that time, hovering over the dunes, he covered an actual distance of only 120 feet (36.6 m).

Orville Wright with the plane equipped with his automatic pilot, partly visible above and behind his head. In the air, when the plane's position changed, the mechanism took control and returned it to level flight.

A NEW HOUSE, A BROTHER DIES

Early in 1912, the brothers were planning a large new home in a well-to-do area of Dayton. They named it Hawthorn Hill, after the elegant hawthorn trees on their hilltop building lot. Wilbur cared little about the plans, saying all he wanted was his own bath and bedroom, but Orville took charge of every detail. When painters couldn't mix the exact red stain he wanted for the woodwork and doors, he did it himself. Heating, plumbing, and wiring were all installed from his own designs. As in many large houses, rainwater was piped from the roof into a cistern, but Orville invented a filtering system that cleansed the water of odor, color, and sediment. When he found the carpet's border not quite in line with the living-room fireplace, he sent the carpet makers in Ireland his own drawing of how it should fit. They changed the border.

Early in May, before the new house was ready, Wilbur felt sick and had a fever. At first, his doctor thought he had malaria. Then specialists determined that he had typhoid fever, probably the result of a trip to Boston in late April during which he must have eaten shellfish that were poisoned by sewage. He died on May 30, 1912, at just forty-five years old.

Against the family's wishes, a public funeral was held at the First Presbyterian Church of Dayton, where no Wrights had ever been members. Some 25,000 people crowded in and around the church and, at the end of the half-hour service, church bells tolled throughout the city. On that signal, all Dayton businesses and industry, all automobiles and streetcars and telephone service, and everyone on the sidewalks stood still and silent for three minutes.

Orville Wright leads pall-bearers carrying his brother's casket from the church following the funeral service.

THE RIVER IN THE LIVING ROOM

Orville and Katharine voyaged to Europe in February of 1913 to continue the fight over patents. In England, their lawyers got the government to pay for all wrongful use of the Wright patent. In France, they won a high court decision, but it was appealed to an even higher court, with the appeal expected to last longer than the protection offered by the patent. In Germany, the Supreme Court ruled that, while the Wrights had invented wing-warping, they had lost patent rights because they let the world know about it before they patented it. Orville said that was like saying a pickpocket was not guilty because the victim showed where his wallet was.

While Orville and Katharine were sailing home, Judge Hazel again issued an injunction preventing Curtiss from making, selling, or showing airplanes. Curtiss went to the U.S. Court of Appeals and was allowed to keep operating his business while awaiting its decision.

Back home in March, Orville and Katharine watched heavy rains bring the Miami River, which bordered West Dayton, over its banks. They moved as many books, pictures, and furniture pieces upstairs as they could. By March 26, their longtime home at 7 Hawthorn Street was under 8 feet (2.4 m) of muddy water and the Wrights were forced to visit friends on higher ground. When the flood receded, slimy, thick mud was everywhere, entire neighborhoods were littered with furniture that had floated from homes, and 371 Daytonians were dead.

The Wrights' downstairs rooms were ruined, but in Orville's darkroom in the shed out back, he found his glass photo negatives only slightly damaged. The priceless photo of the first December 17 flight was almost untouched. And in the rear of the bicycle shop, where the flood had been

FIRST LICENSED FEMALE PILOT DIES

By 1910, airplane pilots had to pass tests and earn licenses to fly. The first licensed female pilot, Harriet Quimby, was a Boston newspaper reporter who thought she should learn to fly to help her write about flying. No sooner did she learn than she decided to be the first woman to fly across the English Channel, as Frenchman Louis Bleriot had done. In 1912, using only a compass, a watch, a barometer, and a thermometer as instruments, she flew from England to France. Home again that summer in Boston, she flew passengers—one at a time—before large crowds at an air show. There she lost control when her passenger threw the plane out of balance by shifting his weight. First he, and then she, fell from the plane to their deaths. The seat belt had not been invented yet.

12 feet (3.7 m) deep, the original 1903 Wright Flyer—the only Kitty Hawk plane the Wrights had kept—was safe. Because the pieces gathered after its crash were still in crates, it had been protected by a heavy coating of mud.

The Wright home that was moved from 7 Hawthorn Street in Dayton to Greenfield Village, Michigan. The porch and shutters were built by Wilbur and Orville when they were young men.

TWELVE

INVENTING AUTOPILOT AND A POPULAR TOY

Orville Wright was now president of the American Wright Company. Although its headquarters were in New York, he stayed in Dayton, keeping his office not in the airplane factory but where it had always been—in the bicycle shop.

In October of 1913, the U.S. Patent Office approved the patent for Orville's stabilizer, or automatic pilot. Orville wanted to use it to win the Collier Trophy, awarded annually for the most important development in flying. On New Year's Eve, as judges watched, Orville flew his single-seat Model E around Huffman Prairie seven times, with his arms raised high above the controls.

He won the trophy, but his automatic pilot was soon outdated by the Sperry Gyroscope. The Sperry Gyroscope was actually two gyroscopes, one that controlled roll and pitch, and one that controlled yaw.

SPINNING TO THE MOON

A gyroscope is a wheel that spins inside a frame that holds its position even when moved, just as you can move while a toy gyroscope spins on your fingertip.

In 1911, American inventor Elmer Sperry's gyrocompass (a gyroscope spinning in the same direction as Earth) controlled warships. The next year, his son Lawrence made gyroscopes to steady airplane controls. To prove they worked, young Sperry flew his plane past a grandstand full of judges while he himself stood in the cockpit with his hands in the air and his mechanic stood out on a wing of the plane. The inertial navigation system that guided humans to the moon in 1969 used Sperry's invention.

The U. S. Court of Appeals decided in January of 1914 that Glenn Curtiss had infringed the Wright patent. The directors of the Wright Company thought this meant the company could have a monopoly—that is, complete control—on making airplanes. Orville disagreed. He insisted that anybody could build airplanes as long as they paid the Wright Company a royalty of 20 percent of the sales price for each one. And that meant anybody, he explained, except Curtiss.

TRIES TO MAKE LANGLEY'S PLANE FLY

Curtiss thought he could get around the patent decision by showing that an airplane had been *able* to fly before December 17, 1903, even if it had not actually flown. He got the Smithsonian Institution to provide $2,000 for him to rebuild what was left of Langley's Aerodrome. He put in a more powerful engine, changed the wings' camber, strengthened the wing structure, added pontoons for takeoff from water, and installed his own control system. But on May 28, 1914, near Hammondsport on Lake Keuka, New York, he could not make the Aerodrome fly beyond 150 feet (45.7 m). He began making more changes. In the meantime, the 1914 Smithsonian *Annual Report* announced, without mentioning the changes, that the original Aerodrome had flown "without modification."

Glenn Curtiss flies his modified version of Samuel P. Langley's "Aerodrome" a total distance of 150 feet above the waters of Lake Keuka, New York.

By June of 1915, Curtiss had the Aerodrome ready for another trial. Orville sent his brother Lorin, who would not be recognized as he would, to Lake Keuka. Lorin registered at the hotel as W. L. Orin. On June 3, he watched as the rebuilt Aerodrome barely skimmed the water for 1,000 feet (304.8 m) before its rear wings collapsed. Lorin took pictures, but Curtiss's friends forced him to hand over the film.

Back at the Smithsonian Institution, the Aerodrome was rebuilt to its original 1903 condition and put on display three years later, in 1918. Its label said: "The first man-carrying aeroplane in the history of the world capable of sustained free flight. Invented, built, and tested over the Potomac River by Samuel Pierpont Langley in 1903. Successfully flown at Hammondsport, N.Y., June 2, 1914."

No one seemed to know where the June 2, 1914, date came from. That was a whole year before Lorin watched the Aerodrome's wings collapse on June 3, 1915. On that earlier date, short "flights" had lasted only a few seconds and were so brief that no official measure of time or distance was taken.

A SHORTER DAY AND HIGHER PAY

Factory workers and their bosses were astounded on January 5, 1914, when they learned that the Ford Motor Company had raised its workers' lowest pay rate. It went from $2.40 for working a nine-hour day to $5 for an eight-hour day. Such high pay was unheard of at that time.

The falsehood enraged Orville Wright. Curtiss announced that, since the court said his controls were like wing-warping, he would build planes that used only one aileron at a time to get around the patent. So the Wright Company's New York directors wanted to sue Curtiss again.

Orville disagreed. He bought most of the board members' stock so that he controlled the company. Next, he sued Curtiss himself in November of 1914. Finally, while awaiting court action, he sold the company to a group of New York businessmen for $1.5 million plus a $25,000 consulting fee for the first year. It was more money than he and Wilbur had made while Wilbur lived. At forty-three, he was extremely wealthy.

Orville, Katharine, and their father were now settled in the Hawthorn Hill mansion. There Orville added a Saint Bernard puppy named Scipio to the family and enjoyed watching it grow from 16 to 160 pounds (5.9 to 59.6 kg). Eighty-eight-year-old Bishop Milton Wright died in the house on April 2, 1917, just before the United States entered World War I.

On the grounds of Hawthorn Hill, Orville Wright plays with his devoted Saint Bernard, "Scipio."

Now friends of Orville organized the Dayton-Wright Company, with him as consultant, to build four hundred training planes and four thousand bombers for the U.S. Army. In May of 1917, Huffman Prairie and other vast pastures around it became the army's Wilbur Wright Field. The army made Orville Wright a major in the Aviation Section of the Signal Officers Reserve Corps, but he stayed in Dayton and never wore a uniform. His job, he later said, was to keep American engineers from making unneeded changes in the De Havilland 4 bombers they were building from British designs. He also helped design and build the Kettering Bug, a pilotless bomb-carrying robot biplane named for Charles F. Kettering, a friend of Orville's who had developed the self-starter for automobiles. On its third test, the Bug—without explosives aboard—took a wild flight of 21 miles (33.8 km). When it was found after dark, farmers with lanterns were wondering why they couldn't find its pilot.

THE UNITED STATES GOES TO WAR

Beginning in the summer of 1914, the Great War (later to be known as World War I) raged in Europe between France, England, and Russia on one side, and Germany, Austria-Hungary, and Italy on the other. The United States was considered to be neutral, taking neither side. On May 7, 1915, however, a German submarine sank the passenger ship *Lusitania*, killing 1,198 people, of whom 128 were American. The sinking angered countless Americans. Diplomatic protests and negotiations by the U.S. government were unable to keep the United States out of the war, and on April 6, 1917, Congress declared war on Germany.

MILLIONS DIE OF INFLUENZA

Just as the Great War was ending, an epidemic of influenza swept the world. Far more severe than the common cold, it produced symptoms such as headache, backache, and high fever. Middle-ear infections, bronchitis, and pneumonia often resulted. It was estimated that in 1918, the epidemic took the lives of 20 million people worldwide, including 548,000 in the United States.

The war ended before the Bug could be perfected. The idea of pilotless planes did not come up again until Nazi Germany flew unmanned "buzz bombs" into England during World War II.

FLIPS AND FLOPS

After World War I, Orville continued thinking in his laboratory. Once he noticed that two boys had climbed a tree to peer in a window near which he was working. He got a chuckle out of hearing one boy tell the other, "He's inventing."

Soon he developed an idea he had had since 1914: the slotted wing, a cambered strip that increased lift so the pilot could slow his plane during a dive. In 1922, the U.S. Navy said it was useless. But twenty years later, in World War II, pilots flying the navy's Douglas Dauntless dive bombers were glad they had it.

In 1923, Orville devised a toy whose spring sent a wooden clown through the air to be caught by another clown in a swinging trapeze. Called Flips and Flops, it was Orville's only profitable invention after World War I. When sales slowed, the manufacturer made toy gliders. Orville designed and built a machine that cut the balsa-wood parts as well as a press that imprinted advertising messages on them.

Katharine Wright was elected to the board of trustees of Oberlin College, where she had been president of the Alumni Group, in 1923. Also on the board was Henry J. Haskell, associate editor of the *Kansas City Star*, an Oberlin classmate who had once been Katharine's math tutor. They had kept in touch over the years, and now romance developed. In 1925, fifty-one-year-old Katharine became engaged to marry Henry, but she didn't tell Orville. She wanted to wait for the right moment, and in 1925 her brother was too busy with non-family matters.

Orville's fight with Curtiss had ended in 1917, when the entire aviation industry agreed to pool its patents. But the Smithsonian Institution still claimed that Langley's plane had been *able* to fly before the Wrights flew. More and more, the world believed that Langley had been first in flight.

FIRST TRANS-ATLANTIC FLIGHT

At Rockaway, on Long Island near New York City, three of the U.S. Navy's Curtiss flying boats took off on May 6, 1919, to cross the Atlantic Ocean. Refueling stops were planned in Newfoundland and the Azores. One plane became lost in fog and was abandoned at sea. Another landed on seas so rough it could not take off again. The NC-4, however, not only reached the Azores, but flew on to Portugal and England. Altogether, including stops along the way, the trip took three weeks.

LENDS 1903 FLYER TO ENGLISH MUSEUM

In a speech in England in October 1921, however, Orville's friend Griffith Brewer revealed how the Aerodrome had been rebuilt at Lake Keuka, so it was not the same as the original. The speech jolted aviation experts who had believed the Smithsonian Institution, but the institution's secretary said nothing.

Orville waited until 1925. Then, convinced that history would credit Langley with inventing the airplane, he announced that he was lending the 1903 Wright Flyer—the one in the famous photograph, the same one that had survived the flood—to England's Science Museum of London. "I believe that my sending our Kitty Hawk machine to a foreign museum," he said, "is the only way of correcting the history of the flying machine, which by false and misleading statements has been perverted by the Smithsonian Institution."

VISITORS COME, SISTER GOES

Katharine had waited for one year for the right moment to tell Orville she was getting married. She finally told him in the summer of 1926. He was dumbfounded. He could not believe that his Sterchens would leave their brother-sister life. He refused to attend the wedding, held at Oberlin College in November of 1926. He wouldn't even talk to her.

Orville now had Hawthorn Hill to himself, except for his beloved housekeeper and her husband, who were live-in help. His nieces and nephews and their children visited often, and now and then came special visitors.

Stopping in Dayton while flying across the United States after his successful solo flight from New York to Paris, Charles A. Lindbergh is greeted by Orville Wright.

One was Charles A. Lindbergh. Orville invited him to stay overnight at Hawthorn Hill after his New York to Paris solo flight in May of 1927. He landed the *Spirit of St. Louis* at Wright Field on June 22 on his way to St. Louis. The two bashful pilots wanted a quiet dinner at the mansion, but they had to respond when a mob trampled the Hawthorn Hill grounds and crowded onto its porches. The horde departed only after both men appeared on a balcony above the front portico.

Katharine and her husband made their home in Kansas City. In February of 1929, she became ill with pneumonia. Orville, who had not communicated with his sister since before her wedding, was told how sick she was, but he refused to go to Kansas City until Lorin insisted. He was with her when she died on March 3, 1929.

The next year, a visiting writer from *The New Yorker* magazine described Orville as "a gray man now, dressed in gray clothes. Not only have his hair and his mustache taken on that tone, but his curiously flat face. . . . A timid man whose misery at meeting you is obviously so keen that, in common decency, you leave as soon as you can."

Major magazines were now running articles with headlines such as "Bring Home the Wright Plane." More and more people thought Orville Wright was a victim of the powerful Smithsonian Institution. And in 1937 he drew his will. It said the 1903 airplane was to stay in London after he died unless he later filed a letter saying he had changed his mind.

During those years, Orville's mind and hands constantly tinkered with mechanical things. To hear music, he built his own automatic record changer, but his family teased him about the number of records it broke. In his car he installed heavy-duty shock absorbers to ease the bumps that pained his back and leg, both sore ever since the Fort Myer crash. He took apart his secretary's brand-new electric typewriter to see how it worked, but then had to call a serviceman. But when several Dayton jewelers said his complex ship's clock was beyond repair, he fixed it himself.

A 1940 visitor was President Franklin D. Roosevelt, who was campaigning for his third term and running against Republican Wendell L.

FIRST WOMAN TO FLY ACROSS THE ATLANTIC OCEAN

Amelia Earhart first became famous when—not yet a pilot herself—she flew across the Atlantic Ocean as a passenger on June 17, 1928. Praised for such courage, she said, "The bravest thing I did was to try to drop a bag of oranges and a note on the head of an ocean liner's captain—and I missed the whole ship!"

Willkie. He invited Orville to ride with him in a parade through Dayton. The president's car then headed back to Hawthorn Hill. At the foot of the long, winding driveway, Orville asked the chauffeur to let him out. He didn't want to take the president out of his way.

END OF SMITHSONIAN FEUD

In 1942, newswriter Fred Kelly contacted Charles Abbot, secretary of the Smithsonian Institution. It was time, he said, to publish the differences between Langley's 1903 Aerodrome and the 1914 Lake Keuka machine, and to deny the untrue claims made about the plane. Abbot agreed, publishing an announcement approved by Orville Wright. It said the 1914 Aerodrome tests had not "proved that the large Langley machine of 1903 was capable of sustained flight carrying a man."

ELECTED PRESIDENT FOUR TIMES

Franklin Delano Roosevelt, who was known as "FDR," was the only U.S. president elected to four four-year terms. Until 1940, the tradition was that a president who had served two terms did not try for a third. In that year, however, after FDR had been leading the country's fight to overcome the Great Depression of the 1930s for eight years, the Democratic Party nominated him to continue in office. He was re-elected. His fourth nomination and election came in 1944, when the country was in the midst of World War II and his leadership was needed more than ever. Soon after his fourth inauguration, however, on April 12, 1945, FDR died of a stroke.

With bombs falling on England, the 1903 plane had been stored underground. Orville wrote to the Science Museum saying he wanted the machine returned when the war ended, but his letter was not made public.

The year 1943 brought the fortieth anniversary of the first flight. Top military officers, U.S. congressmen, and members of Roosevelt's cabinet invited Orville to a celebration in Washington. Orville gave Secretary of Commerce Jesse Jones permission to announce that the 1903 Wright Flyer would be returned to the United States after the war, and told him that he would come to the anniversary party only if he didn't have to take part in the program or speak.

At the dinner, Jones announced the Flyer's future return. Then he double-crossed Orville Wright, asking him to present a trophy to General "Hap" Arnold, who had been Orville's student at Huffman Prairie. Without

At the dinner celebrating the fortieth anniversary of the first flight, Orville Wright presents the Collier Trophy—awarded annually "for the greatest achievement in aviation in America"—to General H.H. "Hap" Arnold. Orville had taught Arnold to fly at the Wrights' flying school. Here, he participates in a three-way handshake with Arnold and U.S. Secretary of Commerce Jesse Jones (center) despite his shy reluctance to participate in the program.

saying a word and without smiling, Orville stepped forward, handed Arnold the trophy, and sat down.

FIXING A DOORBELL

In October of 1947, late for lunch with a friend, Orville raced up the steps of a Dayton building and collapsed from a heart attack. He recovered and was told to slow down.

Three months later, the doorbell at Hawthorn Hill didn't work. Orville spent a morning fixing it, hurrying up and down the cellar steps to get parts, and stepping in and out of frigid weather. Later, at his laboratory, he had his second heart attack. He lived for four days more, dying on January 30, 1948. In his wallet, his nieces found a thirty-one-year-old photo of Scipio, his beloved Saint Bernard.

During Orville's funeral, Dayton schools and city offices closed. The minister said he was "a man who was just one of folks like us—middle-class, mid-Western American." Above the cemetery, four jet fighter-planes zoomed in a five-plane formation, showing one empty space.

Orville Wright left a fortune of more than $1 million, most of it to his nieces and nephews and their children. He willed $300,000 to Katharine's cherished Oberlin College and smaller amounts to his boyhood pal, Ed Sines, and to mechanic Charlie Taylor.

Executors of Orville's will found the letter he had written to the Science Museum in December of 1943: "I have decided to have the Kitty Hawk plane returned to America when transportation is less hazardous than at present." They let the Smithsonian Institution buy the priceless relic for $1. The museum had to agree to exhibit it only in the Washington area,

The 1903 Wright Flyer hangs today in the Smithsonian Institution, where it was permanently installed on December 17, 1948.

to display with it the label the executors wrote, and to give the machine back to them if the Smithsonian Institution ever recognized any other plane as having been capable of controlled and sustained powered flight with a man aboard before December 17, 1903.

At just after 10:00 A.M. on December 17, 1948, exactly forty-five years after mankind's first powered flight, the Kitty Hawk Flyer was officially installed in the Smithsonian's North Hall. Its permanent label reads:

THE ORIGINAL WRIGHT BROTHERS AEROPLANE

THE WORLD'S FIRST POWER-DRIVEN

HEAVIER-THAN-AIR MACHINE IN WHICH MAN

MADE FREE, CONTROLLED, AND SUSTAINED FLIGHT

INVENTED AND BUILT BY WILBUR AND ORVILLE WRIGHT

FLOWN BY THEM AT KITTY HAWK, NORTH CAROLINA

DECEMBER 17, 1903

BY ORIGINAL SCIENTIFIC RESEARCH THE WRIGHT BROTHERS

DISCOVERED THE PRINCIPLES OF HUMAN FLIGHT

AS INVENTORS, BUILDERS, AND FLYERS THEY

FURTHER DEVELOPED THE AEROPLANE,

TAUGHT MAN TO FLY, AND OPENED

THE ERA OF AVIATION

TIMELINE

THE WRIGHT BROTHERS' LIVES   WORLD EVENTS

1867 Wilbur Wright is born on a farm near Millville, Indiana, on April 16.

1871 Orville Wright is born in Dayton, Ohio, on August 19.

1874 Katharine Wright is born at 7 Hawthorn Street on August 19.

1879 Thomas Edison invents the electric light.

1889 Orville publishes his weekly newspaper, the *West Side News*. On July 4, mother Susan Wright dies.

1890 Wilbur and Orville publish their daily newspaper, *The Evening Item*.

1892 The Wright Cycle Shop opens for business in December.

1898 Marie and Pierre Curie discover radium.

1900 In September, Wilbur travels to Kitty Hawk, North Carolina, and Orville follows three weeks later. They take turns flying aboard their glider.

1901 Wilbur addresses the Western Society of Engineers. The brothers use a spinning bicycle wheel and then a wind tunnel to experiment with wing designs.

1902 In August, after changing the shape of their airfoil, the brothers return to Kitty Hawk, add a movable rudder, and fly twice the length of a football field.

1903 Orville and Charlie Taylor build the first Wright engine. Orville makes the first powered flight on December 17.

1904 The Wrights make test flights at Huffman Prairie and at Kitty Hawk.

1905 Wilbur flies 24 miles (40.6 km) in 39 minutes.

1906 The U.S. Patent Office grants the Wrights' patent on wing-warping.

1908 On September 17, Orville is severely injured and Selfridge is killed in the Fort Myer crash.

1909 In January, Orville and Katharine join Wilbur in France and meet royalty at Pau, then travel to Italy and England. In June, they return home to a celebration in Dayton and then are received at the White House. In October, one million New Yorkers see Wilbur fly over the harbor to Grant's Tomb, and the American Wright Company is created.

1910 The Wrights start flying schools and enter the flying exhibition business. Wright exhibition pilots injure spectators and are killed in crashes.

1911 Orville goes to Kitty Hawk to test his automatic pilot in October.

1912 The brothers plan their Hawthorn Hill mansion. Wilbur dies of typhoid fever on May 30.

1913 Orville and Katharine go to Europe to fight to protect their patent.

1914 The U.S. Court of Appeals decides that Curtiss infringed the Wrights' patent. Orville sues Curtiss.

World War I begins.

1917 The United States enters World War I.

The Dayton-Wright Company is established and signs contracts to build Army planes for World War I. The Huffman Prairie area becomes the U.S. Army's Wilbur Wright Field.

1918 World War I ends on November 11.

1923 Orville invents his successful Flips and Flops toy.

1927 Charles Lindbergh crosses the Atlantic Ocean in his plane, the *Spirit of St. Louis*.

1929 On March 3, Katharine dies of pneumonia in Kansas City.

Worldwide economic depression begins.

1932 Amelia Earhart is the first woman to fly solo across the Atlantic Ocean.

1937 Orville draws his will, leaving the Wright Flyer in London unless he later says otherwise.

1939 World War II begins.

1940 Orville accompanies President Franklin D. Roosevelt on his campaign parade through Dayton.

1943 Orville attends the Washington celebration of the fortieth anniversary of the first flight.

1945 World War II ends.

1948 Orville dies of a heart attack at age seventy-six on January 30.

TO FIND OUT MORE

BOOKS

Freedman, Russell. *The Wright Brothers: How They Invented the Airplane*. New York: Holiday House, 1991.

Joseph, Paul. *The Wright Brothers (Inventors)*. Minneapolis: Abdo & Daughters, 1996.

Old, Wendie C. *The Wright Brothers: Inventors of the Airplane*. Berkeley Heights, NJ: Enslow Publishers, 2000.

Parker, Steve. *The Wright Brothers and Aviation*. New York: Chelsea House, 1995.

VIDEOS

The Age of Flight: Kitty Hawk. MPI Home Video, 1990.

Biography: Wilbur and Orville: Dreams of Flying. Arts & Entertainment (A&E) Television Networks, 1994.

The Winds of Kitty Hawk. Fries Home Video, 1989.

The Wright Stuff. Koch Vision/Shanachie Video, 1996.

ORGANIZATIONS AND ONLINE SITES

The Henry Ford Museum & Greenfield Village
20900 Oakwood Drive
Dearborn, Michigan
http://www.hfmgv.org

This is the home page of the Henry Ford Museum & Greenfield Village. In the 1920s, automobile manufacturer Henry Ford began collecting nearly one hundred notable American buildings and preserving them at Greenfield Village, near Detroit, Michigan. The Wright home and bicycle shop were moved from Dayton to Greenfield Village in 1937, and are open to the public.

The Smithsonian National Air and Space Museum
http://www.nasm.si.edu

This is the Web site for the National Air and Space Museum, where the 1903 Wright Flyer is on display.

U.S. Air Force Museum
1100 Spaatz Street
Wright-Patterson Air Force Base
http://www.wpafb.af.mil/museum

Links take you through the history of the Air Force, beginning before World War I. You will also find links to early pioneers of flight and to each year of the Wright brothers' work from 1900 to 1910.

The Wright Brothers Aeroplane Company & Museum of Pioneer Aviation
http://www.first-to-fly.com

This Web site includes links to a variety of information about the Wrights.

A NOTE ON SOURCES

Writing this book made me feel as if I were living with the Wright brothers for many months. That feeling grew from reading the several excellent books about the brothers that have been published in recent years. The most interesting and complete biography is Tom Crouch's *The Bishop's Boys: A Life of Wilbur and Orville Wright*. It provides far more details of their lives and work than can be included here.

Another very useful book is Fred Howard's *Wilbur and Orville: A Biography of the Wright Brothers*. A book that is not as detailed as the first two but that captures the spirit of the Wrights' adventures is *Kill Devil Hill*, written by Harry Combs with Martin Caidin. For background on aviation's first fifty years, I turned to my favorite book on the subject, *Song of the Sky*, written by Guy Murchie.

I found other good specific details in *The Road to Kitty Hawk* by Valerie Moolman. The clearest and most understandable illustrations and photographs are in the beautiful book *On Great White Wings*, by Fred E. C. Culick and Spencer Dunmore. The most complete source of the Wright brothers' own words is the big fat two-volume *The Papers of Wilbur and Orville Wright*, edited by Marvin W. McFarland.

While writing this book, I turned almost constantly to my thirty-volume *Encyclopedia Americana*, which was published some fifty years ago, in 1953. I find it invaluable for research on any subject that dates before then. It contains mountains of detailed information that is likely to have been left out of more recent encyclopedias to make room for up-to-date information. Among the countless subjects I traced in the encyclopedia were the bicycle, typhoid fever, the Outer Banks, the Smithsonian Institution, wood engraving, photography, ready-to-wear clothing, the telegraph, the U.S. Patent Office, the U.S. Lifesaving Service, and many more.

The World Book Encyclopedia, 50th Anniversary Edition, was also valuable for the same reason. For many specific, up-to-date, and historical facts, I relied on *The World Almanac and Book of Facts 2001*, a book that is always at the corner of my desk.

Then there was the Internet. Searching on *Google* took me within seconds to such subjects as hockey, *Collier's*, *Scientific American*, *Popular Science*, *Manufacturer and Builder*, *The Century*, and *McGuffey's Readers*.

—*Bernard Ryan, Jr.*

INDEX

ABOUT THE AUTHOR

Bernard Ryan, Jr., has been an aviation buff ever since he saw barn-storming pilots take passengers aloft in open-cockpit biplanes from a neighboring farmer's field. He has authored, co-authored, or ghost-written twenty-eight books. His *Tyler's Titanic* is an early chapter book about the adventures of a boy who finds a way to visit the wreckage of the great ship on the ocean floor. His *Helping Your Child Start School* is an introduction to kindergarten for parents. *Simple Ways to Help Your Kids Become Dollar-Smart*, co-authored with financial planner Elizabeth Lewin, helps parents teach children, ages seven to eighteen, how to handle money. His *The Poisoned Life of Mrs. Maybrick* is the biography of an American woman who, in Liverpool, England, in 1889, was the defendant in one of history's great murder trials. The books in his eight-volume *Community Service for Teens* cover *Caring for Animals; Expanding Education & Literacy; Helping the Ill, the Poor, & the Elderly; Increasing Neighborhood Service; Participating in Government; Promoting the Arts & Sciences; Protecting the Environment;* and *Serving with Police, Fire, & EMS.* His first published book was a career guide for young people, *So You Want to Go into Advertising.* Mr. Ryan has written many shorter pieces for magazine and newspaper publication and is the author of one hundred reports on courtroom trials published in three major reference books: *Great American Trials*, *Great World Trials*, and *Sex, Sin and Mayhem: Notorious Trials of the 1990's*. He is a graduate of The Rectory School, Kent School, and Princeton University. A native of Albion, New York, he lives with his wife, Jean Bramwell Ryan, in Southbury, Connecticut. They have two daughters and two grandchildren.